SOUNDINGS

Anita Brookner

SOUNDINGS

THE HARVILL PRESS
LONDON

First published in Great Britain in 1997 by
The Harvill Press
84 Thornhill Road
London N1 1RD

3 5 7 9 8 6 4 2

The publishers are grateful for permission to reproduce the following illustrations:
p.2 Théodore Géricault, *Monomanie du vol* (Museum voor Schone Kunsten, Ghent);
p.18 J.A.D. Ingres, *Paganini* (Cabinet des Dessins, Musée du Louvre); and
p.32 Eugène Delacroix, *Paganini* (Phillips Collection, Washington)

A CIP catalogue record for this book is available from the British Library

ISBN 1 86046 388 6

Designed and typeset in Dante at
Libanus Press, Marlborough, Wiltshire

Printed and bound in Great Britain by Butler & Tanner Ltd
at Selwood Printing, Burgess Hill

700
887

Contents

Acknowledgements

Anita Brookner is grateful to the editors of the *Times Literary Supplement* and the *London Review of Books* for permission to reprint articles that appeared in those journals in the 1970s, 1980s, and 1990s. Above all she is grateful to the Courtauld Institute of Art for the years she spent there. The three lectures on Géricault, Ingres and Delacroix were originally delivered in the beautiful Adam room that was then part of the Institute's home at 20 Portman Square.

SOUNDINGS

Théodore Géricault, *Monomanie du vol*

I

Géricault

CHARLES CLÉMENT, A LIKED and respected figure in the world of Paris belles lettres in the 1850s, became art critic for the *Journal des Débats*, in succession to the formidable Delécluze, in 1863. Monographs on artists, usually no more than extended essays, were the order of the day, and there is a great deal to be said for that simple form. Clément published studies of Leonardo, Raphael, Michelangelo, Poussin, Decamps and Gleyre, and they are scrupulous, worthy and tenderhearted. In 1862 he turned his attention to Géricault: a monograph and *catalogue raisonné* appeared in 1867, and both are surprising on two accounts. The first is that despite the ensuing age of zeal the work has never been superseded, and the second is Clément's curious confession in his introduction, which begins, *"C'est en tremblant que j'ai commencé cette étude. Je n'ai jamais été autant effrayé, et je le dirai, affligé du sentiment de mon impuissance . . ."* This is an oddly fervid and even neurotic statement from a man whose emotions had previously given evidence of having been put into excellent order and control by the calming influence of Lake Geneva, where he grew up and attended school and university.

The reason he gives for this trembling, this affliction, is a feeling of inability to do justice to the greatest artist of his time. But in fact his malaise can be felt by anyone brave enough to reopen the Géricault dossier. For throughout Géricault's work there runs a thread of psychic darkness strong enough to twist the most prepared nerves and

standing forth for all to see today in the crusted bitumen of the great
Salon canvases or the lattice-like drawings, which must be handled
with extreme care, because the fierce ink has bitten through the paper,
and the threat of disintegration is very real. Violence, secrecy and
despair emanate from these fragments, and these conditions are still
palpable. Clément's trembling was justified, for his subject was indeed
awesome. And Clément's prophetic words go some way to explaining
the fact that the definitive Géricault biography has not yet been
written, and indeed may never be written, for it demands the qualifica-
tions not only of an art historian but of a painter, not only of a classical
scholar but of a humanist expert in the mutation of forms, not only of
an archivist but of a specialist in manic depressive states.

It is when one tries to match up the facts as recounted with the
pictures as painted that one runs into difficulties. For throughout
the relatively few works that Géricault drew and painted during
his brief career he seems alive to an element of danger which cannot
be explained away in purely circumstantial terms. The *Wounded
Cuirassier*, who shows no signs of physical damage, sinks quietly to the
ground, gazing upward and in vain for a source of light. Carabineers,
eloquent in their reproachful silence, emerge from black night like
two-dimensional versions of Hamlet's father's ghost. The victims on
the *Raft of the Medusa*, who were in fact exposed to the full blaze of the
tropical sun, toil towards salvation and the brig *Argus* like victims of
some hypothetical mining disaster. The *Epsom Derby of 1821* is run
under a sky swollen with thunder clouds. A Montmartre *Lime Kiln* is
shown at nightfall, with a farm cart wedged into an impossibly
small doorway. A monster child, *Louise Vernet*, lolls inertly in a menacing indigo landscape. Into all of these works are built patterns of
alarm more informative than the studies of rearing horses or snarling
tigers to which much attention has been paid, as if they alone gave
a clue to the savagery of the painter's disposition.

This dark current, so different in quality and association from that

"bon noir", that *"heureuse saleté"* that Delacroix tried to capture in the
Massacres at Chios, runs like a groundswell through Géricault's art until
it reaches open expression in the portraits of the dead and the insane.
Yet so perfectly is it expressed in terms of subject-matter, so easily is
it identified with a mood of historical anti-climax (the *Wounded
Cuirassier* of 1814 is said to be "about" the French defeat in Russia), that
the mind finds it simpler and more satisfying to accept such generalizations. But painting, as Delacroix understood, while exercising the
eye, really subsumes and operates on the whole complex of memory
and association behind it. By this standard Géricault's pictures offer
nothing less than experiences of dramatic terror.

Yet the story Clément tells begins quietly enough. Géricault was
born in Rouen in 1791, the only child of a well-to-do family with
Royalist sympathies. This last detail conveys an impression of conventional thinking, unswayed by the propaganda of the Revolution. The
troubles of the period seem to have been absent from the house in the
rue de l'Avalasse where Géricault grew up, surrounded by a full
panoply of grandmother, mother and father, and aunt and uncle,
whose name was Carruel de Saint-Martin. These mundane facts are of
great importance. When his mother died, in 1800 or 1801, his young
aunt, Alexandrine de Saint-Martin, who was a mere six years older
than Géricault himself, took the mother's place, and we may assume
the family connection to have been a close one because, also at this
date, Géricault's father, Georges-Nicolas Géricault, entered into a
business association with his brother-in-law Saint-Martin, possibly as
a gesture of appreciation for his wife's caring role.

By 1799 the family had moved to Paris. There Géricault attended
various schools with a Royalist bias, ending up at the Lycée Impérial, a
Napoleonic institution, where he seems to have been under the influence of a teacher of overt Royalist sympathies named Castel. He too
plays an important part in the story. Géricault was not academically
inclined; he spent all his spare time at the circus and the riding school,

hoping that people would mistake him for a jockey. He left school in 1808. Against the wishes of his father but with the help of his uncle he entered the studio of Carle Vernet, an agreeable but superficial painter of horses and hunting scenes who did nothing to feed Géricault's demanding and subversive imagination, although Vernet's influence is resurrected in many of the works executed later in England.

In 1810 Géricault went to a second master, Pierre-Narcisse Guérin, who was of much greater use to him. At first sight they appear to have little in common, for Guérin is a Neoclassical painter of no great originality, particularly adept at the noble profile and the rigid stance. Yet Géricault's mature work is stamped with two decisive influences: that of middle period David, with his commitment to contemporary events, and that of the classical tradition, which can be seen at the heart of all Géricault's more ambitious works. It was this latter tradition that he absorbed in Guérin's studio. A shop sign painted for a blacksmith in Rouen at about this date could not be more humble in destination, and yet the attitude of the horse presupposes a knowledge of Coustou's *Chevaux de Marly*. This is perhaps the earliest example of Géricault's ability to absorb or appropriate a sculpted or engraved original. It is only fair to suppose that this ability to incorporate a classical or pseudo-classical source depends on the kind of instruction that Guérin was known to dispense.

There is additional evidence of the weight of Guérin's teaching in several drawings which deal with classical subject-matter in a clean linear manner very different from his later drawings, which seem to be devoted to the principle of energy. Certain manuscript notes from this period have survived, including a timetable which Géricault drew up for himself, in which the key word is *"antiquités"*. The so-called Zoubaloff sketchbook in the Louvre contains a number of pencil notations inside the back cover, addresses of men who sold antique medallions, and the note *"gravures Homère"*, which can only allude to the English artist Flaxman's engravings from the *Iliad* and the *Odyssey*, immensely popular in Paris in the last decade of the eighteenth century and first decade of the nineteenth. In this same notebook Géricault states his intention of perfecting himself in music and Italian. The handwriting is elegant, and it must be said that at this date there is no sign that Géricault is to be anything but an accomplished minor master.

But by 1811 or 1812 the emphasis begins to change, for at this date he starts to frequent the Louvre, which had then reached its point of maximum enrichment before Napoleon's defeats reversed the traffic of masterpieces from conquered or annexed European countries to Paris. Clément cites a number of copies made by Géricault after a wide choice of masters: Titian, Raphael, Caravaggio, Poussin, Rubens, Van Dyck, Rembrandt, even a near contemporary such as Prudhon. Some radical process takes place in these copies: the influence of Guérin recedes and the painter takes over from the draughtsman. In particular a study after Titian's *Entombment* shows him to be intent on capturing the dramatic quality, and, more impor-tant, the tragic quality, of the original. This is more than competent work: it has a freedom of handling one could hardly have been led to expect from a novice constrained by a classical education. Already the mature Géricault is visible in the sweep of the outlines and the dark suffused colouring. The element of loss, so significant a component of Géricault's later work, is overwhelmingly present.

In 1812, a fatal date in France's history, Géricault made his début in the Paris Salon, for it was always his ambition to be an accepted master, an ambition which his unorthodox enthusiasms did little to serve. To the Salon of 1812 he sent only one picture, the huge *Cavalry Officer Charging*, a brilliant fiery luminous work, executed in a rapid and open manner to which in fact he never returned. The extreme tension, mobility, almost desperation, of the *Cavalry Officer* are unusual in Géricault, who is normally a painter of single figures seen in telling isolation. Also unusual is the predominantly red harmony of the colour scale. Unlike Gros, whose portrait of Murat hung opposite the *Cavalry Officer*, Géricault was not painting a patriotic subject; his work has no ideological basis. Anecdote has it that the composition was suggested by an incident which took place on the road to Saint-Cloud in September 1812, when Géricault drew a grey horse rearing with fright. His friend, Robert Dieudonné, an army officer, posed for the figure; when Dieudonné was no longer available the Royalist Count D'Aubigny took over. Legend also has it that the picture was executed with great speed, and the fact that the Salon opened on 12 October lends weight to this. But the surface of the picture is heavily worked, so heavily worked that the horse stands out in something like low relief, while obvious pentiments can be read by anyone viewing the picture in a raking light. It was well received, was awarded a gold medal, and was bought by the state. Géricault never repeated his early success, nor does his paint ever again display this ferocious energy.

Indeed the *Wounded Cuirassier Leaving the Field of Battle*, which he sent to the Salon of 1814, seems weighty and immobile by comparison with the earlier work. By 1814 news of Napoleon's defeat in Russia was known in Paris, and the picture was badly received, possibly because it showed a French officer in an unheroic light. Critics noted with some disappointment that Géricault had apparently regressed to a slower and more deliberate execution, and treated the picture as something of a false start, although the heaviness is entirely characteristic. The *Cuirassier* contains greater depths of thought than the earlier picture, and, in the gloved hand grasping the sword, more passages of beautiful paint. Clément makes the point that the picture is about defeat: *"les jours mauvais sont venus"*. It may be rash, however, to assume that Géricault is painting in terms of defeat in the purely historical sense. With very few exceptions all his works are about defeat, even when they purport to illustrate victory or deliverance, as in *The Raft of the Medusa*.

The *Cuirassier* won no medal and was not bought by the state, and these facts intensified in Géricault the form of agitated depression which was to take so dangerous a turn in 1819. His reaction was a desire to get away, and towards the end of 1814 he took the extreme step of joining those Royalist forces that were to act as the King's bodyguard. Whatever his reasons for this extravagant and profession- ally unhelpful gesture, he was soon overtaken by events, because on 5 March 1815 Napoleon landed at Golfe Juan from Elba, his temporary exile, and marched on Paris. The King, Louis XVIII, decided on retreat; Géricault accompanied him to the Belgian border, where the troop was disbanded. Like his own Cuirassier Géricault left the field almost furtively, abandoned his uniform, and lay low until it was safe to return to Paris. This explains why very few paintings can be ascribed with certainty to the years 1814–16.

A more significant journey took place in October 1816, when Géricault travelled to Italy at his own expense. A great deal of thought went into this project, because he undertook, before leaving, a complete inventory of his pictures, notebooks, palette and colours, all of which he handed over to his father for safe-keeping. This indicates that he had in mind a fairly lengthy stay. Yet he was not confident enough to travel alone, and beseeched various friends to accompany him. None, as it happened, was available. He arrived in Florence in the middle of October 1816, stayed about a month, and made drawings after Michelangelo's Medici tombs, of which he was to retain a power- ful memory when he came to paint the figures on the *Raft of the Medusa*. He wrote a number of letters to his friend Dorcy in Paris, complaining of sadness and irritability, and hinting at "troubles" in which he had imprudently involved himself. This indicates, or refers to, the adventure which was to culminate in the birth of his son in 1818. However, if Géricault had envisaged his journey to Italy as a partly justified flight from a dangerous situation he was not able to maintain his resolve, for when Dorcy wrote that he was at last able to join him Géricault replied, without explanation, *"Je suis obligé de partir,"* and added that he was leaving behind his easel, paintbox, and a few primed canvases. This contrasts strangely with his meticulous preparations for his earlier departure from Paris. Also, when his luggage was unpacked after his return it was found that more than twenty oil sketches for his projected masterpiece, *The Race of the Riderless Horses*, were there, but they had been put into the box so hastily that they were stuck together. This detail is significant, as is the fact that Géricault left behind, or otherwise abandoned, the huge canvas on which he had begun to paint *The Race of the Riderless Horses*, and which could no longer be found in 1867, when Clément was writing his book.

Although this canvas no longer exists, there are a number of small studies of men restraining horses which were obviously intended for a giant panorama, perhaps inspired by the Elgin Marbles, of which he had seen casts made available to him by a sculptor friend. It is interesting to speculate on what the final canvas would have looked like. Had it been a frieze, as seems likely, it would have been an attempt to impose a classical appearance on what was in reality a popular riot, the race along the Corso in Rome, which took place every year. But it was never finished, or, more probably, was never even started.

It is at this point that Géricault's story takes on a darker and more tragic dimension. By November or December of 1817 he was back in Paris and reunited with his mistress. On 21 August 1818 their son was born and was registered as being of father and mother unknown. The father was of course Géricault himself. It is now accepted that the mother was Géricault's aunt, Alexandrine de Saint-Martin, the woman who cared for him after his mother's death. Clearly there is material here for every conceivable type of guilt. And indeed Géricault's fatalism and instability crystallized around this relationship, with more or less final consequences. Two strange landscapes, dating from this time, reveal significant morbidity in their details of drowned bodies and dismembered hands. No rational explanation for these is available.

The year 1818 also marks the inception of a period of greater ambition, when Géricault began to search for a theme for a formal finished composition to be exhibited in the Salon. His breakdown after the subject he finally chose, *The Raft of the Medusa*, and its cold critical reception, reveal the depths of his desire to be recognized and patronized, for despite his outstanding gifts he had as yet made no mark on the artistic situation of his time. His cast of temperament militated against a judicious, pondered, intellectual assessment of what material might or might not be appropriately translated into pictorial terms. He made a spectacularly false start with a series of drawings illustrating a famous murder case of the time, the Fualdès affair. Fualdès, a politician from Rodez, was dragged away from his home some time in 1817, and taken to a local brothel, where his throat was cut. His body was thrown into the river, but not before his blood had been fed to a pig. The reasons underlying this *cause célèbre* are not known. Equally mystifying is Géricault's idea that it would be acceptable in an official setting. He abandoned the project when a series of popular lithographs made it superfluous. It may be that he intended to exploit this particular market for himself, for in 1817 he began to experiment with the lithographic process. Technically brilliant, he mastered it with apparent ease, and it was to be his main source of income when he came to London.

With the affair of the *Medusa* he was on stronger moral ground. This was a genuine horror story which dominated French opinion and which had recognizable causes and effects. In the summer of 1816 the frigate *Medusa*, captained by a former émigré, whose only qualification for the job was loyalty to the Royalist establishment, was proceeding to the colony of Senegal with the governor and the colonial administration on board. On 2 July the ship struck a sandbar in the Indian Ocean, and the crew and passengers took to the lifeboats. As the ship had been improperly provisioned, both lifeboats and rations were found to be inadequate: 149 men were forced to pile onto a raft which was to be towed by one of the boats. However, in order to ensure their own survival, the men in the boat severed the ropes towing the raft, which drifted for twelve days. The men on the raft succumbed to heat-stroke, starvation, cannibalism and madness. On the twelfth day they managed to attract the attention of the brig *Argus*. Of the 149 men on the raft fifteen survived, among them the ship's main engineer, Corréard, and the ship's doctor, Savigny. On their return to Paris these two men published an account of the affair.

Géricault's friend Auguste Brunet, a sociologist and political economist, introduced him to Corréard and Savigny, a meeting that was evidently crucial. Géricault, having found his subject, went to great lengths to ensure that his understanding of the *Medusa* débâcle was detail-perfect. Not content with the verbal and written testimonies of Corréard and Savigny, he commissioned the ship's carpenter, who had also survived, to build him a small replica of the raft. He went to Dieppe to study the waves. The installation of his replica raft meant that he had to move to a larger studio. He found one near the Hôpital Beaujon, and this apparently contingent action was to have spectacular results, because in his desire to study extreme physical and emotional deprivation as close to the model as possible he began to visit the dissecting room of the hospital, became friendly with doctors and custodians, and in a very particular sense explored the world of physical death, not as an outsider but almost as a partici-pant. The studies made after human remains – and these would have been guillotined heads in the first instance – have a horrifying empathy, as if the painter were somehow involved in the preceding agony. The mutilated fragments are still eloquent with a sense of the anterior life and personalities of the victims. A dismembered arm and leg lie together like lovers in a bed, while the male and female heads have the same sense of passionate dialogue abruptly cut off. The paint is eerily beautiful, as if no means were too perfect for the facts of death, yet the physicality of the process is unmistakable.

To turn from the revelation of these inspired and terrible works, in which Géricault speaks without prompting from his teachers and predecessors, to the finished exhibited *Medusa*, with its debts to Michelangelo and David, demands a slight adjustment of one's critical faculties. Géricault had no innate gift for complicated large-scale composition, and the many preliminary studies for the picture are descriptive exercises mainly concerned with the relation of the raft to the picture space. These are finely drawn and washed in with an overall loose-wristed movement, whereas the final work is built up in quasi-sculptural blocks, controlled by, or obedient to, a system of grids and diagonals, the method by which David worked. The appearance of the finished picture, too, has more than a little to do with David, for Géricault is reported to have taken time off to study David's *Leonidas*, and the same note of tragic striving, almost the same gestures, are present in the two works. This tragic quality transforms the figures on the raft, which are basically a series of academies, and gives the picture its overwhelming power. As the picture is painted, and as it has to be hung, the spectator is on the raft; the spectator identifies with the dead and dying at the bottom of the canvas rather than with the figure at the top; the spectator cranes his head to keep it above the water-line. His deliverance, the *Argus*, is so tiny that it is almost invisible, and in fact the *Argus* passed by without noticing the raft; it was only on its second sweep of the area that it made contact. The spectator is by no means persuaded that the *Argus* will arrive in time, or even that its arrival will be relevant to the devastation that has already taken place.

Géricault spent eight months on the actual painting of the *Medusa*, shaving his head for what was undoubtedly an ordeal, or, as it proved to be, an execution. His assistant, Monfort, describes him standing on a table, painting in complete silence from first light to nightfall, deeply disturbed by the slightest noise or movement around him – Monfort was obliged to wear carpet slippers. He made much greater use of the model than hitherto, and many friends and acquaintances were pressed into service in the morgue-like studio. When the picture was transported to the Théâtre Français, where the Salon of 1819 opened on 25 August, Géricault noted that the lower right-hand corner was uncomfortably empty, thus emphasizing the tilt of the raft. In a few days, according to Clément, he brushed in the figure of the shrouded nude, thus anchoring the picture more satisfactorily, and adding a final touch of pathos to this disturbing work.

The picture finished, Géricault invited his former master Guérin to view it. Guérin, who obviously had reservations, nevertheless gave it an hour of his time, a gesture which Géricault appreciated. The general public was far less impressed, refusing to find, much less to look for, originality. Ingres reacted violently, and in later life demanded that it be kept out of sight so as not to corrupt the taste of the young. In the main the *Medusa* was found offensive; the inability of the establishment critics to concentrate on the subject of the picture – which by universal consent was described as a shipwreck – was probably motivated by a general desire not to antagonize the government and the official exponents of government views. Critics therefore tended to look at details of colour and execution, and their descriptions are more or less irrelevant now that the paint has sunk and the excessive use of bitumen become more obtrusive. The experience depressed Géricault profoundly. The rest of his life was punctuated by attempts to sell the picture to the state, although it was quite obvious that official silence on this matter was complete. The only compensation that Géricault received was a commission to paint a *Sacred Heart of Jesus*, laughable in view of the fact that he had never painted a devotional picture in his life. The commission was passed on to Delacroix, whom Géricault paid for his trouble. The finished work is now in the cathedral at Ajaccio.

The ardour with which Géricault had undertaken and executed the *Medusa*, and the indifference with which it was received, had predictable results. He left Paris, threatened by his most serious nervous depression to date. It is at this point that Clément's admirable narrative falters and can be amplified by more recent research. Clément gives no account of the time that elapsed between the exhibition of *Medusa* and the arrival in London in the spring of 1820, yet a self-portrait in Rouen, showing Géricault with hair *en brosse* and a disquieting expression, impels us to concentrate on his vicissitudes in those crucial months. Within the relatively recent past a French scholar, Denise Aimé-Azam, has discovered valuable letters that passed between Géricault's friends, including his former schoolmaster Castel, describing his instability, his excitement, his desire to paint, and his disabling fear that boatmen on the river near Castel's house in Fontainebleau had been sent to take him away. It is Mme Aimé-Azam's excellent theory (which cannot, however, be substantiated) that Géricault's friends were obliged to have recourse to a young man specializing in obsessional neuroses, the excellent Dr Georget, that Georget removed Géricault to his clinic in the rue de Buffon, and that Géricault there painted the miraculous heads of the insane, who were in fact his fellow sufferers. Great mystery surrounds this episode, and has created the equivalent of the San Andreas fault in the chronology of Géricault's works.

The traditional and more cheerful explanation for these canvases is that after a successful trip to England Géricault returned to Paris in good order and painted for his friend Georget ten portraits (only five are extant) to illustrate a forthcoming treatise on alienation. There are several reasons for not accepting this view, the most practical being that drawings or engravings, or, even better, lithographs would seem to be a more appropriate medium for this kind of illustration. Moreover, on his return to Paris, Géricault was suffering from many ailments, notably a disease of the spine, and in fact painted relatively little; even his drawings weaken noticeably.

But perhaps the most convincing argument lies in the execution of the portraits of the insane: painted with extreme rapidity, without retouches, and in a state of unflinching empathy, they correspond with the state of excitability and delusion for which Mme Aimé-Azam's letters provide slender but convincing evidence. It would have been difficult to use these portraits in a didactic work, for they show no attributable symptoms; they are merely faces of people sunk in terror, suspicion or bewilderment. The titles by which they are known are not contemporary. There is no attempt to interpret the minds of these people, or to illustrate their condition in a public way. Accessories, like the child molester's hat (*Fou voleur d'enfants*), worn in fact like a child's schoolcap, are in no sense explanatory to the lay spectator. The klepto-maniac (*Monomanie du vol*) has a face of great beauty, with eyes sunk in innocence and doubt. The woman characterized as *Monomanie de l'envie* is not bending her mind in any recognizable direction. In view of this evidence – or lack of evidence – it is reasonable to assume that the portraits were painted at the lowest point of the descending curve triggered off by the public failure of the *Medusa*.

The journey to England in 1820 was undertaken partly for therapeutic reasons and partly for commercial ones. An impresario named Bullock put *The Raft of the Medusa* on public exhibition in the Egyptian Hall in Piccadilly, where it drew crowds and received a favourable notice in *The Times*. His confidence thus restored, Géricault began to concentrate on new subjects, and also on making money, chiefly through the medium of lithographs, his best work at this time. He painted and drew anodyne subjects, ladies riding in the park, ostlers, the Derby, but also a public hanging, and members of the urban poor. He set out to learn what he could from painters such as Wilkie and Landseer, and he began to find fault with the French school. A rather unexpected desire to make a fortune began to be noticeable, and on his return to France he started to invest unwisely, and to sink money into an enterprise for making artificial jewellery, possibly in the sinister little building known as *The Lime Kiln*.

He had already tried to kill himself in London, and a melancholy now distorts his work. Projects were sketched but abandoned as too demanding; magnanimous advice and help were offered to Delacroix; and the very few pictures that he finished exude sadness in their turbid paint and their irrational darkness. Louise Vernet, who was to become a beauty and to marry the painter Delaroche, is portrayed as a cynical child clasping a cat. Her waved hair has a grossness that suggests that the paint was difficult to move. Similar distortions of scale are present in the Louvre picture known as *Le Vendéen*, also an approximate title. The sitter is probably a dressed-up model and any disharmony conveyed by the painter himself. The grotesque black hat extinguishes the sitter's face like a candle-snuffer. He wears a dark blue coat and a light brown waistcoat, striped a pinker brown with the brush. His glistening white shirt is arbitrarily arranged to expose a rhomboid of dark blushing flesh.

Géricault's death is equally sinister. Returning from the jewellery factory one morning, he fell from his horse onto a pile of stones. An abscess developed which he opened with his knife; the infection accelerated and he was soon bedridden. On 16 May 1823 he managed a visit to Delacroix's studio, looking very ill, as Delacroix noted. He died at the beginning of January 1824, the year of the great Romantic Salon, in which Constable showed *The Hay Wain* and Delacroix *Scenes of the Massacre at Chios*. He was thirty-three years old.

Delacroix dressed grief and despair in acceptable colours, whereas Géricault did nothing to make these conditions palatable. Even a superficial reading of his paintings will give an impression of unusual subject-matter further distorted by the internal pressures by which the artist was to transcribe mental states, without ever faltering in his struggle to be an epic modern master.

J.A.D. Ingres, *Paganini*

2

Ingres

INGRES, A FORMIDABLE TEACHER, made strenuous attempts to indoctrinate his pupils, not only by his own example but by uttering precepts so dire that one has the distinct impression that they should have been carved in stone and handed down to posterity. Among his prohibitions were personal ambition, invention, and bright colour, which he considered unhistorical and in any event disloyal to the spirit of the ancients and of Raphael. He did nothing to disguise the fact that he considered himself to be their direct descendant, and saw nothing impertinent or even unhistorical in so doing. Fortunately while Ingres was trying hard to be one thing, a passionless and serene nineteenth-century ancient, his temperament was arranging for him to be something quite different, a portraitist of outstanding modernity and a painter of fantasies which drew uneasy tributes from Baudelaire, who found them shocking. He is at one and the same time the most traditional and the most revolutionary of painters: behind the auto-crat lurked an innovator who now appears more radical than his rival Delacroix, his superior in self-knowledge, his inferior in transparency.

His links with his immediate past present no problem. He owes much to his master David and to his fellow students Girodet and Gérard. He has considerable claims to be regarded as the earliest French Pre-Raphaelite, the French Nazarene, the most massive French genius of his time to give support to that form of dainty archaism derived from Flaxman and in these years applied largely to small genre pictures about the home life of famous historical or literary characters. One should take very seriously his emphasis that the most desirable quality that the true artist should possess is naïveté, for this links him with the longing for purity and regeneration that is the legacy of the late eighteenth to the early nineteenth century. One should also take very seriously his notorious and substantial rivalry with Delacroix. Although there may now be more admirers of Ingres than of Delacroix, this was not always the case. In their own lifetime Delacroix was regarded as the painter who made all the important discoveries of his generation, while Ingres was limited by his provincial background, his limited education, and his own obstinacy. Ingres was constrained in fact by being nothing but a painter, while Delacroix was considered to be a man of the world, a sophisticated Parisian, courteous, mysterious, handsome and well-connected. In the contest of appearances Delacroix won easily, and since their rivalry was comprehensive this too is a factor to be considered.

Ingres can indeed appear limited, perhaps because of his curious mixture of didacticism and unworldliness. There is an aspect of Ingres which can be equated with lesser manifestations of nineteenth-century academicism: the faultless nudes in airless settings, the antique love scenes played out in dizzying areas of painted marble, the portraits of overpowering people. This is certainly a less endearing but by no means worthless side to Ingres. There is also his contemptuous attitude to the appeal of a picture, to colour and harmony, the sort of attitude that led him to say that the technique of painting could be mastered in a week but the study of drawing demanded a lifetime. There is his defiant belief that the capital of Europe was still ancient or Renaissance Rome rather than nineteenth-century Paris. There is all the tyranny of exact prototype and categorical pronouncement, of the deliberate and sustained backward glance, the tyranny of rules and of obedience to rules, the sheer unfaltering confidence that he was in all cases right. Ingres at all times worships the orthodoxy of form;

he does not speculate as to what lies within that form. This makes him both a very literal painter and a curiously devout one.

This rigorous personality was allied with a singularly sanguine temperament, the sort of temperament that made his female nudes too plump, too passive, the sort of temperament that was beguiled by decoration, by hair, by jewels, by contemporary dress. The true oddness of his make-up can best be illustrated by the National Gallery's portrait of *Mme Moitessier Seated*, and his tyranny by the history of the commission, which he received in 1844 from M. Sigismond Moitessier, a wealthy banker. A delay immediately set in. By 1849, with a general design of Mme Moitessier and her daughter Catherine agreed upon and even laid in on the canvas, Ingres was further immobilized by the death of his wife. In 1851 the tenacious patience of his patrons finally forced him to paint a fairly rapid portrait of Mme Moitessier, one that departs from the original formula, on another canvas. This work, now in Washington, shows a large, moody and authoritative woman about to go out for the evening. Anchored to the floor by a pyramidal dress of black Chantilly lace, her head surrounded by a wreath of pink roses, she is every rich businessman's evidence of conspicuous consumption and expenditure. Only the tensely out-thrust fingers of the pink glove on the chair give an indication of almost furious boredom, a symbiotic boredom in which Ingres and his model joined, for even though he was willing to paint her again he was dissatisfied with the pose.

In 1856, having dismissed first a dark dress, then a yellow one, Ingres encased Mme Moitessier in a stupendous flowered creation and returned her to the pose of a Roman goddess from a Herculeaneum wall painting, to which he had first likened her almost twelve years earlier. The model is almost as awe-inspiring as the master himself. Mme Moitessier gives off such a resonance that one can sympathize with the susceptible Baudelaire, who, when facing a room filled with paintings by Ingres, felt as if all the oxygen had been sucked out of the atmosphere, leaving him threatened with syncope. Hating yet admiring the untroubled sexual balance of Ingres, and his curious lack of self-doubt, Baudelaire was, by his own admission, made uneasy by the spectacle of feelings no less powerful than his own but completely antithetical to them.

George Sand, who unhesitatingly took the side of Delacroix in the great dispute, dismissed the portly, incoherent Ingres out of hand. Delacroix, who certainly knew better, described him as "merely clever". Merely clever? It was Ingres, the expert violinist, who depicted Paganini, in a badly fitting greatcoat, as an amiable entertainer, and Delacroix who painted him as a demented embodiment of the devil's trill. Whose was the received idea here? It was Ingres who portrayed Liszt as potentially angelic and Gounod as ineradicably well-groomed. As he himself put it, in a letter to Pauline Gilibert, he was "morally young", and with this moral youthfulness went an unimpaired keenness of appreciation, an undiminished awareness of the erotic aura given off by the women he consented to paint. For though he professed to loathe portraits they were his main source of income; he reasserted his independence of his sitters by his despotic slowness of execution. Apart from this he appears to have loved his benign and healthy sitters, to have invested them with something of their own self-satisfaction, to have offered them, with their fullest cooperation, what Henry James calls "occasions of homage". Such homage is an undisguised perception of the nature of their sexuality. This was the characteristic that unnerved Baudelaire.

As a young man in David's studio Ingres was allowed to paint the lamp in the master's portrait of Mme Récamier. She, like Mme Moitessier, was the beautiful wife of a wealthy banker. Yet there is a world of difference between David's Mme Récamier, vulnerable, and, beneath her sophisticated trappings, uncertain, and Ingres' Mme Moitessier, who appears to be in possession of all worldly knowledge. She sits in her crowded boudoir with her famous finger to her temple, dominating with ease her challenging dress. Her gaze is both remote and replete; its descent from the Mona Lisa is not difficult to trace. At first sight it is an arrogant work. Yet on further contemplation the hard-edged image seems to fade and become more opaque, and Mme Moitessier undergoes a transformation from upper-class fortune-teller to Delphic oracle. Nor is this merely a matter of contrasting the personality she presents to us with her mirror image, that not quite accurate reflection seen in a glass darkly, as if the other side of her were in a different room. By concentrating on the shadowy depths of the portrait, and laying emphasis where it is least expected, Ingres endows the foreground with a disconcerting opacity. Central to the confusion of meanings is the door off to the left, a door through which no one will ever enter or leave. There may also be a message in the detail of the tiny putto on the sofa frame, with his despairing glance towards the relatively mountainous Mme Moitessier. The final impression she gives is of a woman to whom life has been more than kind, but whose experience has set her apart from mundane or routine satisfaction. She is as isolated, in her different way, as Mme Récamier.

This dimension was on the whole lost to Ingres' contemporaries. The upholstered sofa, the firescreen, the fan, the Japanese vase, and above all the ring and the bracelets, were condemnatory evidence of the painter's impenitent attachment to the bourgeois world. What is the point of M. Ingres? queried Baudelaire, and answered his own question by stating that here was an antique ideal tricked out with modern accessories. Baudelaire also thought he perceived an indifference, but as a portraitist Ingres is not indifferent; he is sophisticated. He has the titanic patience of the perfectionist, dedicated to the difficult task of rendering what is already perfect, for, as Baudelaire said, Ingres chose his sitters, and they had to conform to an already established ideal. No temperament, added Baudelaire, misled by the apparent absence of second thoughts. Yet he concedes the pain felt by Ingres, although he does not specify its cause. The sheer task of posing the model was for Ingres a supreme and often punishing intellectual exercise. That achieved, and the contour established, he saw no further cause for concern. There is little evidence that Mme Moitessier's dress posed an unusual problem. In everything but his pictorial resolutions Ingres knew his limitations: not for him the examination of souls with their dimension of tragedy – that was the province of the unhealthy Delacroix. But Delacroix was significantly right in one respect: there is no intimation of tragedy in this portrait. Ingres and his sitter are apparently unaware that time happens to everyone. There is an innocent assumption of permanence. It is as if the whole complex science of picture-making, so sumptuously deployed in this work, has been subsumed into the solid image of Mme Moitessier and her challenging dress. Delacroix's irritation is understandable and will be understood by anyone who places his hopes of vindication in an unknown future rather than in a bitter present. For Ingres and by extension his sitters, the present was more than satisfactory. It is a view that only a happy few can share.

Yet Ingres arrived at this unorthodoxy by the most orthodox means. He was a pupil of David, and his emancipation from his rigorous master can be seen in his two portraits of Napoleon. The first, now in Liège and dating from 1804, has the unforced naturalism of the best David portraits of the time, although it is in fact brighter in colour. Yet two years later, when Ingres received a commission to paint Napoleon as Emperor, he sacrificed this naturalism to an icy and doctrinaire image, an icon, in which he outdoes David in ideological zeal, because the model, though not the execution, derives from the archaizing Flaxman, and it is, significantly enough, an outline of Jupiter, Jupiter sending a dream to Agamemnon. The same process can be observed in the early portraits, which, in comparison with those of David, reach an astonishingly rapid maturity. *Mme Rivière* of 1805 exists in an airless compressed world which signals a sensuality that hardly existed for David, and she is given the unmistakable allure of a great cocotte.

David's laconic simplicity has been replaced by a tremendous linear complication; at the same time the importance of sculpture for Ingres is unmistakable. The solid roundness of every form is emphasized, the fluid sinuous pose thrown into high relief by the shadowless clarity of the local colour. The swathe of the shawl over the arm, the fat round curls on the brow, are felt as keenly by the spectator as they were by Ingres himself.

Perhaps evenhandedly he displays his omnicompetence in tackling both portraits and altarpieces, both historical friezes and dangerous modern fantasies. This, he thought, constituted his métier as a classical artist. Yet personal taste obtrudes into the most rebarbative of subjects, into *Oedipus and the Sphinx*, which contains his own self-portrait, into *Jupiter and Thetis*, with its wishfully subservient goddess draped over the knee of an implacable Jupiter (again), into the *Apotheosis of Homer*, overloaded with text yet in fact about the handing on of greatness and therefore of an élite to which Ingres himself was convinced he belonged. If this last belief in the reality of a solemn tradition appears out of date, almost apostolic, the firmness of purpose behind it is difficult to discount. And when the eye declares itself to be exhausted by yet another celebration of primal forces, then there is much to be gained from the very peculiar character of this latter picture, particularly when one reflects that it is a manifesto, that the inarticulate Ingres – famed for his inarticulacy – has chosen this manifesto to express his own beliefs and loyalties. The metaphor becomes clearer in 1850, when Ingres, who liked to revise his earlier work, repeated the figures of the Iliad and the Odyssey who sit on the podium of Jupiter's throne. It can be no accident that the face of the Iliad bears more than a passing resemblance to that of Ingres himself.

He is not easy of access to the modern mind, and for this reason it is possible to do him less than justice. In his lifetime it was the fate of Ingres to be belittled and diminished by the superior taste and sophistication of Delacroix, and to turn from the anguished canvases of

Delacroix to the confident and traditional certainties of Ingres can
be disconcerting. It has to be remembered that the virtues of Ingres
are dramatically opposed to those of Delacroix, not only in a pictorial
but in a human sense. With what gratitude and affection one looks on
the world as perceived by Ingres, a world of recognizable, healthy and
beautiful human beings, unaware of actual or potential flaws, sane,
vital and durable. To view the world as the best of all possible worlds
may be very short-sighted, but it is sometimes very necessary, and it
makes for an easier passage through life. In the first half of the nineteenth century this attitude represents an almost divine optimism, and
this was the conviction which accompanied Ingres throughout his
appropriately long life. He continues a strain of naïveté inherited from
the eighteenth century: he believes, as did the eighteenth-century
reformers, in perfection, in perfectability, and in the infinite potential
for improvement of human material. The sitters whom Ingres painted
in his youth – *Granet, Zélie* – all seem possessed by a delicious secret
confidence in the possibilities of life. But to grow old in this belief, to
defend purity in the knowledge of one's own and the world's impurity,
takes a certain amount of determination. Hence the magnificent
complexity of the mature and late Ingres. The heads in his late portraits seem to contain thoughts which are, to say the least, opaque, but
the heroism of meticulous posing and presentation, the assumption of
attainable perfection, and the desire to put the spectator at his ease, to
literally assure his equilibrium, are still there.

The Homeric Ingres and the pessimistic Delacroix, who considered
modern man to be rootless in a dissolving universe, are beautifully
illustrated in their attitudes to the musician whom each claimed to
understand: Paganini. To Ingres, in a drawing made in Rome, he is
simply that, a musician, an agreeable-looking Italian of no obvious
virtuosity. Only his oversized sleeves indicate his terrible thinness, his
almost skeletal physiognomy, which some saw as a sign of demonic
possession. Certainly Delacroix chose to paint him that way, cramped

and contorted by the fury of his playing, and inclining a furrowed and aged face towards the instrument of his torture. No greater gulf between two sets of perceptions could be illustrated. And it is not only the difference between two sets of perceptions: the technique, or the handwriting, is markedly different. Although the Ingres is an informal drawing it is immaculate, with that thin and infallible line which Ingres considered nobler than effusions of colour. A drawing by Delacroix will be like an explosion of gunshot, indicating energy and unease. A drawing by Ingres will demonstrate that sublime control which he considered to be the obligation of the true artist. By the same token the paintings of Ingres will also be contained within that bounding but unseen line, so that objects are limited, do not spill over, do not merge into one another. A painting by Delacroix will work his unease into the very paint: backgrounds will be unclear, energies diffused, poses in movement, usually of a despairing kind. The great achievement of Delacroix will be to sublimate his own predicaments into an atmosphere of free-floating anxiety which will usually hover over and above his inmost convictions. For this reason there is something of an ambivalence about what he thinks and what he feels. Yet the forms of distress that he chooses to chronicle are so universal that they invariably find an echo in the spectator, although the painter may be performing the task of portraying every reaction except his own.

There are no comparable fail-safe psychological mechanisms in Ingres. Ingres was known to rage and weep until he had found the exact place for everything on his canvas, but once that intellectual problem was solved the picture could be easily, if slowly, finished. So that what he presents is the ultimate solution, not the tentative or existential doubt, and with this solution a triumphant balance, so that the spectator is literally becalmed into tranquillity.

Their travels too are characteristic. Ingres spent the years 1834 to 1841 in Rome; Delacroix chose the more modern destinations of England and Morocco. Morocco yielded a fascination with "unspoilt" civilizations and veiled lives: the famous picture known as *Les Femmes d'Alger*, a harem scene of infinite complexity and overwhelming reclusion, dates from this journey. By comparison Ingres' harem scenes, variations on the theme of an odalisque being serenaded by a slave, although equally complex, have an overt sensuality which owes nothing to the mysterious East. Yet it is evident that Ingres had been looking to more exotic sources than those previously available to him. Despite his fiercely classical loyalties he was not above the temptations of Eastern art, of which he had first-hand knowledge of certain examples: textiles and ornaments in the collection of the painter Gros, Arab and Persian miniatures from the collection of Vivant Denon, Napoleon's minister of fine arts, and more miniatures and carpets in the collection of Italinski, the Russian ambassador to the Holy See, whom he knew in Rome. It is even possible to establish that of the miniatures in the Vivant Denon collection one represented a woman lying on a carpet and another a woman playing a mandolin. Nevertheless the transformation of these sources is courageous, if awkward. The painter's naïveté is revealed in his presentation of these fantasies to the public gaze.

In another picture brought back from Rome to Paris, the *Stratonice* (Chantilly), a picture which had a great success in the Salon of 1840, Ingres beautifully exposes the dichotomy noted by Baudelaire, the antique ideal enlivened with modern accessories. The theme is one much favoured in the eighteenth century: the young Antiochus laid low by a mysterious malady which the doctor Erasistratus diagnoses as a guilty passion for his stepmother Stratonice. The picture is small, virginal, withdrawn: the isolation of Stratonice, based on a Greco-Roman figure of Pudicitia in the Vatican, is recognizable Ingres, but who could have predicted the riot of colour? Stratonice, in lilac, stands in front of a column scarlet to mid height; there is a crimson bedcover, blue drapery on a chair, while the doctor wears blue and the bed curtain is green. The key pattern in the foreground is gold and buff;

on the left it is red, black and white. The whole picture is conceived in
solid blocks of local colour. And because of the lack of complemen-
taries the entire bizarre scheme is rendered curiously bloodless, rather
as if the surface had been drained or dusted. The middle and later
works of Ingres represent not necessarily a decline but an acceptance
of certain tenets of contemporary taste. The architects Percier and
Fontaine used similar colours in their work, most notably in their
plans, while Percier's German-born pupil Hittorf based his entire
aesthetic position on the fact that the architecture of the ancients was
polychrome and produced numerous occasional buildings to illustrate
the fact. One of the most popular, the Cirque des Champs-Elysées of
1833, had yellow columns, blue mouldings, and bas-reliefs on a red
ground. The actual architectural forms of the *Stratonice* are based not
on antique models but on the more colouristic contemporary view
propagated by Hittorf. The bed, for example, almost exactly reproduces the portico of another café in the Champs-Elysées, now known
only from an engraving. Perhaps the nearest extant comparison is the
portico of the church of St Vincent de Paul, near the Gare du Nord,
which was taken over by Hittorf in 1831 and finished by him in 1844.

So Ingres, the *grand bourgeois*, finally found himself at home with
the bourgeois taste of his later years, and this identification was taken
to great heights of achievement in the portraits of the 1840s and
1850s. These magnificent icons, airless, virtually unshaded, pushed up
against the front plane of the picture, show the sharpness of the
painter's eye. They look like photographs and indeed they owe something to contemporary photography. But the peculiar harshness of the
colour, the puce dress worn by Mme de Rothschild, or the strident
blue creation inhabited by Mme de Broglie, are more unsettling than
any photograph. The women dominate; their husbands are nowhere
to be seen. So hyper-realistic are these images that they may induce
a certain nervousness or claustrophobia. One begins to sympathize
with Baudelaire, incapacitated by those triumphant female smiles.

Romantics always get a better press than classicists, largely because there is so much more behaviour to discuss. Delacroix hardly behaved at all, so admirable was his dandyism. He was to many a reproachful figure, whereas Ingres was easier to recognize. Ingres, to the end of his long life, continued to believe in the good things of this world. At the age of eighty-three he painted *The Turkish Bath*, which retains its ability to shock. Based on an impeccable source, the account by Lady Mary Wortley Montagu of women's baths in Adrianople, the second edition of which was published in French in 1805, the picture represents perhaps the painter's dream, a dense group of unrelated nude figures in an atmosphere of voluptuous calm. Revealing in its grossness of appetite, the picture conveys something more complex than erotic exhaustion. Only in the loosely anchored features of some of the faces does Ingres give evidence of his age. The tender shamelessness of the poses is more appropriate to the young man Ingres still knew himself to be.

The last dramatic confrontation between Delacroix and Ingres took place in 1855, when Paris held its great Exposition Universelle. In that exhibition Delacroix showed thirty-six pictures and Ingres sixty-eight. By sheer weight of numbers Ingres won the day, but the battle was inconclusive. Both painters were made Commanders of the Legion of Honour, but the gold medal went to Horace Vernet. The Emperor, seeing that Ingres was suffering dreadfully from the rebuff, rapidly promoted him from Commander to Grand Officer. Delacroix was still misunderstood, or rather not understood at all, by the general public. Nor were official bodies any kinder to him. He became a member of the Institut de France only in 1857, after having presented his candidature seven times. But Delacroix had reason to feel hopeful, for from 1855, the date of Baudelaire's panegyric, his fame was to increase. Ingres, one feels, was happier to have his reward in this life. Yet his posterity was enormous: Manet and Degas would have been unthinkable without him, as would Flandrin and Henri Lehmann.

And although both men might well have repudiated their successors, they would each, in their very different ways, have gained a measure of satisfaction from the knowledge that their teachings and examples had become an integral part of the great tradition.

Eugène Delacroix, *Paganini*

3

Delacroix

EVER SINCE BAUDELAIRE LAID his deathless but morbid imprint on Delacroix, scholars have been deprived of a normative approach to this most terrifying of painters. For if they lack Baudelaire's eccentricities and obsessions, his desire to worship, to seek moral catharsis in aesthetic satisfaction, to accept as revelatory Delacroix's lapidary but obfuscating remarks about art, they are faced with a heavy task indeed, and one which may end in disappointment. Many commentators have fled to the opposite extreme and have tried to impose a pseudo-scientific approach. They have analysed Delacroix's colour theory (which is in fact fairly conventional); they have added mediocre portraits to his *œuvre*; they have examined his views on art, only to conclude that these were fairly widely shared at the time. His *Journals* have yielded little in the way of explanation for his singular and ultimately tragic temperament.

In short, between Baudelaire and the rest there is a deep chasm in which the true significance of Delacroix, sometimes glimpsed, more often rejected, remains obscure. For art historians cannot justifiably lay claim to Baudelaire's *"impeccable naïveté"*, the quality that led him to choose a new pen and to confess to a childlike happiness when writing the name of Delacroix, the idol at whose feet he off-loaded his burden of physical shame, and to whose pictures he attributed a mystic sense of release from the loathed corporeality that dogged his existence. Surprising as this may be, a valid approach to Delacroix is hard to achieve, an approach comprehensive enough to contain both the considerable volume of written and painted evidence that Delacroix has left us, as well as the extraordinary and pervasive torment that he tried so scrupulously to conceal. This is why Delacroix scholarship begins with Baudelaire and is vulnerable whenever it diverges from his conclusions, even though his conclusions do not fit many other people's perceptions and are indeed remote from any agreed norm.

The 1827 *Death of Sardanapalus* is a case in point. Anyone contemplating this crucial work for the first time will experience the following sensations. First and foremost he will receive intimations of sexual experience which carry a distinctly disagreeable charge. The spectator will perceive on the canvas an arrangement of shapes, colours, and spatial configurations which, although logical, and logically worked out, is deeply irrational.

He will instinctively try to equate this with the story the picture purports to tell, a story cast in bad dramatic form by Byron in 1821. In Byron's text Sardanapalus, the Assyrian king, seeing that the enemy is at his gates, instructs his favourite concubine to set a torch to the bed on which he lies, surrounded by all his considerable possessions. Doubt will then set in. For in the Byron text the concubine Myrrha begs to join Sardanapalus on his funeral pyre, thus ensuring a tragic but emotionally satisfying conclusion. But Delacroix shows us an isolated and deadly Sardanapalus contemplating a writhing holocaust of figures who seem to be begging for his intervention but not receiving it. The dark ghost reclining on a tilting bed is impervious to their emotion and is literally entranced not so much by what is taking place in front of his eyes as by what is taking place inside his head. Thus the picture and the text do not match. Moreover the image and the charge it projects are discrete.

The spectator will then perceive on the canvas a disjunction of scale which almost threatens his balance. The figure of Sardanapalus

is small, dusky, remote, while the slaves and concubines are almost
life-size, and so tumultuous that they might erupt into normal space.
In addition, the movement of the picture is diagonal; it is from upper
left to bottom right, and it is impelled by a series of red patches
and flares which leak out of the lower corner like blood. This feeling
of wetness – quite deliberate, for we have the letter Delacroix wrote to
his colour maker asking for the paints to be mixed more liquidly than
those supplied at this date to any other painter – erodes even further
the lack of air already apparent within the confines of the picture.

Clearly something awful is going on, and the task now is to establish
the deliberate arrangements made by the painter to convey an impression of shock. The Byron text, the letter to Haro, the colour maker,
the various sketches and drawings leading up to the finished picture
will all be of help here. But over and above all these elements there is
something more puzzling to be elucidated, namely the unwilled
element that carries Delacroix's own personal meaning and which is
clearly of primary importance. How is this to be interpreted?

Baudelaire perceived, empathetically, no doubt, that the picture
was about impotence. He described this with subtle and scrupulous
obliqueness in the sonnet beginning, *"Je suis comme le roi d'un pays
pluvieux,"* having already laid clues for his reader by stating that a
final judgement on a picture could be a sonnet or an elegy. It is to
be assumed that such an interpretation was not to Delacroix's taste,
particularly as the poem is almost embarrassingly faithful to the
image:

> *Je suis comme le roi d'un pays pluvieux,*
> *Riche, mais impuissant, jeune, et pourtant très vieux*
> *Qui, de ses précepteurs méprisant les courbettes,*
> *S'ennuie avec ses chiens comme avec d'autres bêtes.*
> *Rien ne peut l'égayer, ni gibier, ni faucon,*
> *Ni son peuple mourant en face du balcon.*
> *Du bouffon favori la grotesque ballade*

Ne distrait plus le front de ce cruel malade;
Son lit fleurdelisé se transforme en tombeau,
Et les dames d'atour, pour qui tout prince est beau,
Ne savent plus trouver d'impudique toilette
Pour tirer un souris de ce jeune squelette.
Le savant, qui lui fait de l'or, n'a jamais pu
De son être extirper l'élément corrompu,
Et dans ces bains de sang qui des Romains nous viennent,
Et dont sur leurs vieux jours les puissants se souviennent,
Il n'a su réchauffer ce cadavre hébété
Où coule au lieu de sang l'eau verte du Léthé.

Impotence may be translated as a form of ennui, or the inability to feel no matter how violent the stimulus. References in the poem to the ladies of the court or the spectacle of a bloodbath can hardly be accidental. Once this evidence is admitted it adds considerably to the picture's unease.

On further examination it becomes clear that the disjunction of scale corresponds to the hybridization of the rules of composition advocated by Stendhal and Victor Hugo, and that the detachment of the Sardanapalus figure has its parallels in the plight of those young Romantics who had been denied the excitement of Napoleonic involvement and had merely inherited the weary compromises of the restored Bourbons. Balzac stated that what Napoleon had accomplished with the sword he would emulate with the pen. The same disappointed grandiosity informs the *Sardanapalus*, replacing action with the alternative potency of sublimation.

If Delacroix had not focused our attention so unremittingly on his own feelings, discussion could restrict itself to matters such as possible Hindu sources for the head of the elephant at the foot of the bed. But Delacroix, as he stated most forcefully, intended his art to be a bridge between his own soul and that of the spectator, and his essential genius lies in his masking the meaning of a picture by an image that almost but not quite contains it. This surely is the point of *The Death of Sardanapalus*: a pantomime-spectacle containing a kernel of inalienable truth, and a dissipation of the shock waves thus set up by a cathartic manipulation of paint.

Delacroix's deadly self-knowledge is always combined with a desire to conceal the truth. His writings contain an entire delusional system of contradictory statements which confuse and mislead the reader. Ponderous judgements on High Renaissance classicism are vitiated by his refusal to go to Italy to view such classicism at close range, and are somewhat undermined by the astonishing confession that anything which did not reveal its meaning in an instant was of no value to him. His memory fed on itself and could in fact proceed independently of the thing seen, heard or read. In 1827, when he painted *The Death of Sardanapalus*, Delacroix was still a young man; he had not yet perfected the iron censorship which he was to impose on his predicament. Like the dandy that he was he decided to perfect what could be perfected and to abandon what could not. There were to be no more instances of self-revelation until 1859, when he painted the National Gallery's *Ovid among the Scythians*, the lament of an ageing and eminent figure who sees himself in the fretful pose of a grieving child, a hieroglyph of sorrow all the more poignant in that by 1859 Delacroix could not contemplate either change or consolation.

Delacroix presents one of the great paradoxes of the Romantic Movement, which is in itself a collection of paradoxes. He is perhaps the best example available of the profound changes in behaviour, in understanding, in self-expression, in attitudes to history, to geography and to politics that took place at the beginning of the nineteenth century in all the enlightened countries of Europe but most visibly in France. It has been said that the Romantic Movement in France is a revolt against two people, against Voltaire in literature and against David in painting. However much this statement over-simplifies the problem it does help to establish two facts. Firstly it implies a coupling of literature and painting which is in fact indissoluble. And secondly it suggests that the Romantic Movement was essentially a movement of *contestation*, of protest, one which broke the old rules but only incidentally established new ones. This breaking of the rules, not always a liberating procedure, led in many cases to a feeling of isolation, of rootlessness, of displacement within the universe: between 1789 and 1820 the process of change in France had been rapid, perhaps too rapid. Young men could still remember when the days of the week had had different names, when Napoleon's victories had excited universal ardour, and his final defeat an unwelcome sobriety.

But the singular isolation of Delacroix springs from the fact that he is not only a great Romantic painter, able to encompass both moral and physical conditions; he is the only truly Romantic painter that France ever produced. His predecessors and contemporaries may have painted Romantic pictures; Delacroix alone painted in the style it is still convenient to call Romantic throughout his life, deliberately and consistently and for reasons which he could not perhaps quite explain. His enormous and endlessly enquiring pictorial intelligence, and his quite independent literary gifts, confer on his work a dignity which will always defy complete analysis.

Yet although he was a Romantic painter, an appellation he was quick to repudiate, he was far from being a Romantic personality. He was basically a member of the French upper-middle-class who had received a fairly stringent classical education. His *Journals*, despite the early effusions and confessions, reveal a somewhat restricted and even academic individual, as if the writer, in his later years, were not so much a painter as some kind of elder statesman. This style is not universally available. This is Delacroix's background: the more paradoxical part of his life he created for himself. For one with such a fearless imagination he showed few signs of artistic precocity; in fact he wanted to be a poet. He thought as a literary man, he proceeded as a literary painter, although he strenuously denied this fact, and he was too reflective ever to paint a major picture without an underlying text or thesis. This may be what Baudelaire means when he talks about the morality of Delacroix's paintings: he is referring to the traces of deep reflection that he finds there. And this reflective quality, which reveals evidence of considerable stoicism, and indeed of scepticism, has something classical at its heart. It is the fusion of these two strains – the lucid analytical intelligence and the limitless pictorial enthusiasm – that gives Delacroix his peculiar stature and makes of him such an absorbing, and, in the final analysis, so Romantic a contradiction in terms.

When Delacroix painted his self-portrait in 1821 he defined himself as a newly emancipated artist of the nineteenth century, an intelligent but melancholy Romantic hero-victim, nervous, withdrawn, manifestly too sensitive to withstand the insults he was to receive. Yet in 1839, when he painted a picture of Michelangelo in his studio, he took the overtly autobiographical step of draping his hero with his own neckerchief. Far from appearing at ease in his task, Michelangelo has thrown down his chisel; he sits brooding, in an attitude reminiscent of Dürer's *Melancholia*, that state of inertia that figures in the Romantic vocabulary as spleen, and which, for Delacroix, was the great enemy to which sacrifices must be offered. The frail figure in dusky black of the 1821 self-portrait soon learned to compensate by allying himself with great artists of the past, but as can be seen in the slumped pose of Michelangelo/Delacroix such a process needed continual vigilance if it were to prove successful.

"The mask is everything" is a phrase and an attitude which recurs in the *Journal*. This convention of refusing to embarrass society with the constant imposition of one's inner life is an essentially classical one; it is the classicism of the highly evolved social animal, more common in the seventeenth century than in the Romantic period. Delacroix, the Romantic painter *par excellence*, is, in everything but his painting, a recluse and a reactionary. Despite his admiration for, his devotion, even, to Shakespeare and Byron and Walter Scott, he states in his *Journal* that nothing gives him more pleasure than listening to Mozart and reading Boileau. When, some time in the 1850s, a stranger paid him the compliment that was the kiss of death to any self-respecting nineteenth-century artist – *"Monsieur, vous êtes le Victor Hugo de la peinture"* – he replied coldly, *"Vous vous trompez, Monsieur, je suis un pur classique."* By the same token he refused to acknowledge the repeated critical tributes of Baudelaire, simply because he found the subjective and impassioned quality of Baudelaire's articles tantamount to an emotional indiscretion. When Baudelaire describes *Les Femmes d'Alger* as being heavy with a weight of moral sadness, a sadness contingent upon the condition of original sin, Delacroix, who could not bear to have his motives made explicit, wrote him a chilly little note. Throughout his life Delacroix was to reject the Romantic label with some vehemence, although in a rare indiscretion in the *Journal* he confessed that he was not only a Romantic but had been one since the age of fifteen.

This refusal to descend to the level of the crowd, this fastidiousness and reticence, are counterbalanced by the violence, the whole-heartedness, and the extremism of Delacroix's pictorial imagination. In his various studies of lions roaring and fighting he seems to conceive of himself as a demiurge, as if some vital and elemental contact had been made with the forces of creation, as if he had a view of himself as some sort of instrument or vessel. Enormous control was thought necessary to contain this view.

With his apparent and latent contradictions – his love of energy and his shrinking from commitment, his high social gloss and his pronounced inner solitude, his frequent escapes into the past and his manifestos of contemporary political feeling – Delacroix may be a difficult artist to comprehend. He is also an infinitely attractive artistic personality, perhaps the most glamorous artistic personality since Rubens, with whom he shares so many characteristics. Well born – it is now generally accepted that he was the natural son of Talleyrand, that most Machiavellian of statesmen – highly educated, distinguished in manner, handsome and sought after, Delacroix, like Rubens, presents an image of the artist as man of the world. His artistic ancestry, however, parallels that of Ingres, for both descend from David, Ingres being a direct pupil and Delacroix a pupil of David's contemporary and rival, Guérin. There is, moreover, enough evidence in the early works to show that Delacroix retained certain elements of Davidian classicism and in some ways remained fairly close to David in spirit. The four key pictures of Delacroix's youth – the *Dante and Virgil* of 1822, the *Massacres at Chios* of 1824, the *Sardanapalus* of 1827, and the *Liberty at the Barricades* of 1831 – contain all those life-giving contradictions to which reference had already been made. The *Massacres*, for example, or to give it its full title, *Scenes of the Massacres at Chios*, although painted when he was only twenty-six, contains all the mature Delacroix, and is in addition a handy summary of Romantic enthusiasms and of Delacroix's own methods.

The genesis of the picture is interesting. Firstly, there is something unusual about its subject, which is a fictionalized account of an episode in the Greek wars of independence. The Greek revolt against the Sultan of Turkey began in 1820, and Delacroix's picture commemorates an incident in 1822, when 20,000 Greek civilians were massacred as a reprisal for recent Turkish losses. Delacroix's Hellenism may also be an offshoot of Byron's fame. The thinking behind it is not wholly original. There was a prototype in French painting for this sympathy with the victim rather than the hero and it was one which Delacroix knew very well. This was the masterpiece of Baron Gros, one of Napoleon's official painters, who daringly allowed his own feelings to take precedence over official propaganda. *The Plague Hospital at Jaffa*, painted in 1804, illustrates an event which took place during the Eastern campaign of 1799, when Napoleon visited a plague hospital at

Jaffa in Palestine. This was a sign of heroism sufficient in itself, for Europeans were particularly susceptible to the disease: the young French doctor in the foreground of the picture has just succumbed, and another is blinded by trachoma. But Napoleon does more than expose himself to the infection: he touches the sore of one of the plague sufferers in much the same way that St Louis of France used to touch for the scrofula, the idea being that a recently anointed king possessed quasi-divine powers. So that Napoleon is comprehensively presented as warrior, king and saint, and Gros, who was an ardent admirer of Napoleon, has emphasized the significance of this deed by borrowing a gesture from the iconography of religious painting, the gesture of St Thomas putting his hand into the wound in Christ's side. Marshal Berthier, behind Napoleon, covers his mouth with his handkerchief, as if assisting at the raising of Lazarus. Thus all the associations of the picture refer one, however confusedly, to a sense of the miraculous. Moreover, Napoleon's heroism is underlined by the telling detail of his right hand clutching his glove in an effort to control his repugnance.

This incident did in fact take place. But we know, from an eye-witness account, that Napoleon paid a second visit to the hospital, some three months after the first, that he strode through rapidly, slapping his cane against the side of his boot, and that he gave orders for the very sick to be poisoned so as not to hamper the French retreat. Gros, naturally, commemorated the first visit. So how can there be a connection between Gros' orthodox hymn of praise and Delacroix's lament over the fallen in *Chios*? Perhaps the rather telling fact that Gros, for whom the seeds of Romantic dissidence were to prove fatal, for he eventually committed suicide, has inserted his own opinion on the horrors of war by making the dead and dying figures in the foreground much larger in scale than the otherwise heroic figure of Napoleon who dwindles in stature. And it is precisely these magnificent figures, with their curiously innocent expressions of suffering, and the realism of details like the swelling of the veins in the arms, that Delacroix has made the subject of his picture.

It may be argued that by removing the contrast he has weakened the emotional impact, and that by making explicit and general the mood of despair he has in fact diluted it. David's figure of the dead Marat, isolated on his canvas, may in fact be more poignant than the dying man in the centre foreground of Delacroix's picture who subsides in a comparable pose. Similarly his companion, whose attitude is copied from the figure of Camilla in David's *Oath of the Horatii*, may just be a beautiful supernumerary whose presence is pictorially but not emotionally justified. Moreover, Delacroix has adopted another classical trope: the composition, based on two interlocking triangles, is as rigorously built as any in academic picture-making.

But the *Chios* is also a work of discovery which inaugurates, or rather consecrates, many enthusiasms beyond the range of David. The picture is, for example, of the stature of a Rubens; it sustains an emotional pitch on a tremendous scale; it has the same sense of cosmic significance. More specifically, it is modelled in part on certain Rubensian examples: the horseman and hostage are based on Rubens's *Rape of the Daughters of Leucippus*. But it is in handling that the picture is so resolutely modern, for it has a richness of colour, a softness of glazes, and a sparkle which have nothing to do with Gros or David or even Rubens but are lessons learned from two English painters, Bonington and Constable. Legend has it that when Delacroix saw the pictures that Constable sent to the Salon of 1824 he repainted the sky of his picture on the more naturalistic example of Constable's *Hay Wain*. This would clearly have been impracticable; it seems more likely that he lightened the glazes in the figure groups and added some of those traces of pure white and colour for which Constable was famous. As the picture was cleaned in 1854 this evidence has disappeared, except perhaps for the prismatic tears trickling down the hand of the girl in the foreground. We know about this act of homage to Constable only from the testimony of Frédéric Villot in 1865.

Equally important is the lesson learned from the prodigious Bonington, who brought to France, where he settled in 1817, a precocious and enlightened grasp of the potentialities of the English watercolour technique, and who in his own work translated this technique into oils. The luminosity of the sky in *Chios*, the horse's mane, the turban of the Turkish overseer and the nude torso of the girl are of a lightness of key and handling that Delacroix was to achieve in only one other picture, the *Sardanapalus* of 1827.

Overtones from Gros, from David, overtones from Rubens, references to Constable: these in a sense protected Delacroix with a veneer of old and new mastery. When he came to paint the *Sardanapalus*, which he described as his second massacre, he was not so fortunate or so prudent. The wholehearted sensuality of the second massacre, combined with a certain perverse indifference, outraged official critics and caused the greatest scandal of Delacroix's career. It was thought to violate received canons of taste in its apparent breaking of every rule. Typically enough, for Delacroix's appeal in his own day was in the main to men of letters, it took a poet, Victor Hugo, to perceive the beauty of the painting. Critics were more concerned with its defiant incorrectness.

In a sense Delacroix expressed himself too clearly in the *Sardanapalus* and may have regretted doing so. The retreat into himself might have been even more drastic had he not been given the opportunity to see something entirely new. This occurred in 1832 when he joined the delegation of the Comte de Mornay to pay a six-month diplomatic visit to the Sultan of Morocco. The spectacle of the Arab and Jewish worlds had the effect of freeing him from the last traces of Davidian classicism. He noted defiantly that antiquity was at his door; he was now able to laugh at David's Greeks and Romans. To Delacroix antique now meant unspoilt, prelapsarian, and also colourful, dignified, melancholy, and with the kind of impassivity which he himself was beginning to prize and which he expresses so brilliantly in *Les Femmes d'Alger*. Here too the mask is everything, as the expressionless women merge into their dusky interior. The most obvious influence of the Morocco visit is to supply themes which lasted Delacroix until his death: reviews of troops, beggars, dervishes, battles of Arab horses. A picture of the Sultan Abd-el-Rahman reviewing his troops dates from 1862, that is to say thirty years after the Moroccan experience. The brilliant sunlight of the landscapes and the dim but intense gloom of the interiors affected his colour scale; colours became warmer, harsher, with a typical tonal contrast of reddish-yellow with a deep blue-green. On his return to a colder climate it is the blue-green that comes to dominate.

Yet the classical sense was difficult to eradicate, particularly the classicism of the seventeenth century with which he managed to accommodate his Baroque leanings. However, by the 1840s his style was out of date. The new direction was to be pointed by the realism of Daumier and Millet, a realism with which Delacroix could not come to terms. Fortunately, another artificial break occurred at this time, for he had, mysteriously, succeeded in obtaining a number of government commissions, for which he was more or less obliged to work in a traditional style. These commissions were to occupy the next thirty years, and they were on a vast scale: the Salon du Roi and the Library of the Palais Bourbon, the Library of the Senate, the Galérie d'Apollon in the Louvre, and the Salon de la Paix in the Hotel de Ville. All still exist, with the exception of the Hotel de Ville which was destroyed by fire in 1870. Although faced with awkward shapes and lighting, Delacroix succeeded brilliantly in turning these factors to good account. His ceiling for the Galérie d'Apollon in the Louvre, *circa* 1850, shows the ease with which he worked in a classical setting, taking into account the surround by Lebrun and superimposing his own belated Baroque on to the heroic Baroque of the seventeenth-century master.

The *Journal* tells a more restricted story. The entries for 1857 contain not the slightest reference to the court case arising from the publication of Baudelaire's *Fleurs du Mal*, although for eleven years Baudelaire had been Delacroix's most persistent champion. It is a little difficult too to imagine Delacroix reading *Madame Bovary*, also published in 1857. If he did he made no mention of the fact. Yet the distrust that had plagued Delacroix all through his life had not entirely disappeared. With age came illness, loneliness, and although Delacroix was convinced of his own worth this judgement was not universally shared by his contemporaries, as is shown by his frustrated attempts to become a member of the Institut de France. In 1854 he was turned down for the seventh time. This strange reaction can perhaps be explained by his unique and perhaps unenviable isolation. Despite being widely sought after, both socially and artistically, he gave his loyalty to no one. Good manners, as Baudelaire noted, were a façade for less acceptable feelings.

It is not therefore altogether surprising to find these late years devoted to religious painting of a fairly singular kind. To the Salons of the 1850s he sent four works which mark a new departure in this field: *The Good Samaritan* of 1851, of which Van Gogh made a copy, *The Martyrdom of St Stephen* of 1853 and the contemporary *Supper at Emmaus*, and in 1859 *The Road to Calvary*, bought by the city of Metz, and strongly influenced by Rembrandt. All these works are harsh, dark, expressionistic, a style appropriate, as Baudelaire remarked, to a religion of universal pain.

It is fitting therefore that Delacroix's last work, the decoration of the Chapelle des Saints Anges in St Sulpice, should be a religious enterprise and one in which he achieves a synthesis not only of his own pictorial loyalties but of his imaginative powers. A commission had been offered and accepted in 1849, but there had been a delay when the theme of the chapel was changed. In 1850 Delacroix decided on three subjects: *St Michael Attacking the Rebel Angels*, *Jacob and the Angel*, and

Heliodorus Driven from the Temple. Work went on in difficult conditions until 1861. Delacroix died in 1863.

His increasing classicism can be judged by the influences present in the great ensemble: Michelangelo in the knotted sculptural quality of the figures, Veronese in the sumptuous architecture, Tintoretto in the famous plunging movement. The descending angel in the *Heliodorus* is in fact copied from Tintoretto's representations of *St Mark*. The two great grimy masterpieces on the side walls are difficult to appreciate today; badly lit and discoloured, they are in every sense too big for the chapel which contains them. The *Heliodorus*, which illustrates a scene of divine intervention when Heliodorus was about to pillage the temple at Jerusalem and was stopped, says the text, ". . . by a horse with a terrible rider and two other young men, notable in their strength, and beautiful in their glory, and splendid in their apparel, who stood by him on either side and scourged him unceasingly, inflicting on him many sore stripes". This is perhaps Delacroix's most ambitious personal exercise, but the *Jacob and the Angel* is his noblest imaginative exercise, for it illustrates a peculiarly laconic text: "And Jacob was left alone, and there wrestled a man with him until t he breaking of the day. And when he saw that he prevailed not against him, he touched the hollow of his thigh, and the hollow of Jacob's thigh was out of joint as he wrestled with him." A completely literal reading, made memorable by the furious unenlightened thrust of Jacob and the equally muscular but effortless parrying of the angel, given intimacy by the still-life of Jacob's hat and water bottle, given breadth by the primeval landscape in the dawn light, and given Delacroix's personal signature in the detail of the caravan of servants and animals sent to Esau: Delacroix's last Moorish fantasy.

In 1864, a year after Delacroix's death, Fantin-Latour painted a curious votive picture showing a group of men arranged around a portrait of Delacroix, before which is placed a bouquet of flowers. Those involved in this corporate act of homage are the

painters Manet, Whistler, Braquemond, Balleroy, Legros, Cordier and
Fantin-Latour himself, Baudelaire, and, in the foreground, the man
who gave realism its doctrinal programme, Champfleury. Of these
men only Baudelaire has any direct connection with Delacroix.
The cast could perhaps be modified, filled with Van Gogh, Odilon
Redon, Fromentin and Renoir, with Baudelaire still in pride of place.
For the truth of the matter is that Delacroix's influence on the art
of his time was negligible. The year of his death, 1863, was also the
year of the Salon des Refusés, an event which Delacroix would
have swept aside, in the same way that he paid scant attention to
Courbet and Millet, both of whom visited him in 1854 and received
basically unfavourable comment in the *Journal*. Delacroix, unlike
Ingres, was not interested in teaching; he had assistants but few pupils.
It was left to a later generation to appreciate his unique contribution
to the art of painting.

There is one outstanding exception, Baudelaire, whose obituary
notice of 1863 retraces Delacroix's career with a sympathetic insight
unmatched by any other contemporary testimony. Baudelaire, like
Delacroix, was not concerned with the future of art; both men had a
vested interest in prophesying its decline, but they did so from a truly
genuine position of native greatness. To Baudelaire, Delacroix is the
civilization which is threatened by a new barbarian invasion, of which
the spearhead was represented by the champions of realism. He
underlines, correctly, Delacroix's debts to the generation immediately
preceding him, particularly to David; he also underlines his dependence on literary and historical concepts and ideas. He goes on to
speak of Delacroix's inexhaustible imagination, which enables him
to translate these ideas into a gallery of images. For if Delacroix is in
constant contact with a text his reading of it is always a new one and an
essentially pictorial one. For this reason, says Baudelaire, Delacroix is
the archetypal painter-poet, and on the strength of this quality alone
he is pre-eminent in the history of art. He speaks with admiration of

Delacroix's innate savagery, which he controlled to such an extent that he gave the impression of being a relic of the *ancien régime*, neat, cool, fastidious and sceptical. Hence his curious dualism, a classicist by virtue of his way of life, a Romantic by virtue of his deepest feelings.

Perhaps it is as one of the great pessimists of the age of progress that Delacroix is finally acceptable. In 1863 a new chapter, one of optimism, opened with the Salon des Refusés. Manet and Zola would soon activate the artistic debate. Yet of the two events of that year it was the death of Delacroix that ensured the most decisive break with tradition and the inevitability of a complete change.

4

Rousseau's Social Contract*

THE LAW OF REQUIRED Change, invented by Goethe as a means of classifying natural phenomena, is a useful instrument to apply to certain aspects of social and aesthetic renewal in the eighteenth century. The Law of Required Change presumably called into being the austerity of Neoclassicism from the disarray of Rococo. Art historians can register the change, but without a knowledge of certain theoretical works cannot see by looking why the change was required. Neoclassicism as an aesthetic movement restored the severed connections between contemporary painting and the art, particularly the sculpture, of the Ancients. In a wider context it can be appreciated as the appearance grafted on to the reality of the Enlightenment, that caucus of greatly enjoyable and greatly enjoyed intellectual colloquies conducted by *philosophes*, jurists, moral philosophers, men of letters, theorists of every persuasion, whose faith in the past was only outweighed by their faith in the future.

The painters and sculptors of this period become adept at looking backward to antiquity, but except in the case of David are unable to relate past to future or indeed to present. When they are not copying they are imitating – a function given new respectability by Winckelmann – and in very few cases have their problems, their preoccupations and their priorities any relevance today. Today they seem bound to a historical moment; they can be shown to belong to the

* The Times Literary Supplement, 8 February 1980.

Enlightenment, but there is not much evidence to prove that they understood its wider implications. Hence Diderot's impatience for "a great idea", for great ideas are the Enlightenment's most common currency.

The Enlightenment is also about a new kind of priesthood, a brotherhood of enthusiasts who are demonstrating, through the new gospel of the *Encyclopédie*, that the world is vast and variable, teeming with skills and radical alternatives, a world in which the most important preoccupation is not salvation but a different morality.

The most beguiling conversation of the day is devoted to the question of improvement, or, as it was then called, perfectibility, and it developed around the fashioning of systems – of law, education, government, and in the case of the fine arts, appearance. There was no doubt in the minds of the *philosophes* that mankind would evolve naturally towards these ideal systems, and there was no suspicion that they would or could come about as a result of either revolution or autocracy. These systems had the power of words, not of economics; they were harmless and beautiful and self-justifying constructions, and they did not even aspire to the status of propaganda, because if men were as sensible as they were seen to be in 1760 their natural good judgement would concede that these ideal systems were desirable. The matter could be left there, and evolution would take care of the rest. Who now remembers La Chalotais' *Essai d'éducation nationale*, Mably's *De la législation*, Morellet's *Code de la nature*, or Chatellux's *De la félicité publique*, which ends with the confident statement: "We can assert that legislation, morality and custom have such a hold over our passions that they can bring infinite improvements in the social condition . . . do not let us envy our nephews the precious things that are in store for them; let us enjoy what we have and let us dream the rest"? Who now remembers the Abbé de Saint-Pierre and his project for perpetual peace in Europe? It took him a mere two weeks to formulate in all its ramifications, and he was convinced that it would work. In theory, of course, it does.

It is necessary to accept this confidence in man's perfectibility and this quasi-religious belief in ideal systems to understand not only Rousseau's *Du contrat social* – which is an ideal contract between ideal people – but in order to capture the seriousness of Neoclassicism. It is serious precisely because it is to do with man's desire for perfection, and it is summed up in Rousseau's piercing phrase in *La Nouvelle Héloïse*: "I want to be what I should be." This desire, characterized by Rousseau's biographer, Lester Crocker, as the "ought", led men to aspire to be more generous, more patriotic, more honourable, more constant, more continent, more disinterested, more brave, more noble, more self-sacrificing, more sober, more sagacious, and thus more enlightened than they ever could be. It was the duty of the painters to hold the mirror up not to nature but to the ideal, and to show physically perfect specimens performing morally perfect actions with as little subjective comment as possible from the artist himself, who would thus obey Winckelmann's desideratum that style should be as pure as the purest water. This in itself is an ideal condition.

These desires found a faithful reflection in the painting of the period, of which the finest exemplum is David's *Death of Socrates*. What is lacking in the programme is the equivalent of Rousseau's *Confessions*, a record of those human weaknesses that impel one to take refuge in a theory or a structure. The painters can thus be seen to deal with the hopeful inception of the programme or its stoical conclusion. The human dimension is missing. In the case of Rousseau matters are both the same and different. Rousseau's discovery of the darkness within him made his requirements, both for himself and for society, even more hopelessly ideal than those of his contemporaries. With Rousseau the line of demarcation between philosophy and psychopathology is quite blurred. He was intuitive but not rational; his

mind was brilliant, his memories flawed. *Du contrat social*, his brief
for the ideal state, was published in 1762. In one sense this document
belongs to that brisk tide of publications that would lead men pain-
lessly to Utopia. In another sense it is utterly outside the run of such
systems; hence its notoriety in the early 1760s, when it was burned
by the common hangman in both the Kingdom of France and the
Republic of Geneva.

The obviously rebellious nature of Rousseau's pronouncements, on
art as well as on society, marriage or education, was recognized by the
public from the appearance of his first essay, written when he was
thirty-nine years old and entitled, "Discourse which won the prize of
the Academy of Dijon in the year 1750 on this question proposed by
the Academy: Has the restoration of the arts and sciences been
conducive to the purification of morals?" His answer was that it had
not, a fairly radical position at a time when Mme de Pompadour was
in her heyday at Versailles and handing out commissions of dubious
moral quality, notably to Boucher. Rousseau's particular brand of
contentiousness tends to obscure the fact that his pronouncements
are essentially nostalgic, although the object of his nostalgia may or
may not have existed in fact or in history, a condition in which he
comes interestingly close to Winckelmann. But the one constant that
runs through Rousseau's work – and here he parts company with
the majority of his contemporaries – is that society is a corrupting
influence, and that wherever men are gathered together in cities there
they will corrupt each other.

As far as the Dijon Academy essay is concerned, its apparently
neurotic distaste for high-flown, upper-class, sophisticated and subversive mythological examples is perhaps motivated by Rousseau's
memory of the tools manipulated by his father, who accompanied his
work as a watchmaker with maxims from the classics. As Rousseau
says in his second discourse – on inequality:

I can never recall without tender emotion the virtuous citizen to whom I owe the gift of life. I can still see him, living by the work of his hands and nourishing his soul with the most sublime truths. I see the books of Tacitus, Plutarch, and Grotius mingle before him with the tools of his trade.

In this ideal atmosphere one is to assume that the seeds were sown for later constructs of utility and virtue. But Rousseau, because of his chequered experiences, his absolutely physical need to walk out of a job that humiliated him, and his unique gifts as a writer, considered himself to be equidistant socially from the class of patrons on whom he was in fact dependent all his life, and those simple folk, potential Spartans, to whom he binds himself in principle but with whom he cannot identify. He is the eternal outsider, eternally promoting the claims of what should prevail (the "ought") rather than discussing the reasonable or the possible. His aspirations towards virtue are based on an ancient and ineradicable knowledge that not only is man weak and easily corrupted but that he himself is such a monster of guilt that not even the therapeutic exercise of writing the *Confessions* can resolve, distance, or even neutralize his fears of his own criminality. Rousseau's prescriptive and confessional writings are a measure of his own solipsism: he, and therefore Man, requires models and guides, aids to good behaviour and self-discipline, and so fragile is Man that he will require such support systems all his life, as Rousseau was later to demonstrate in the case of *Émile* and the Tutor. It was for this reason that when Diderot, an agile journalist, suggested that Rousseau stood a better chance of winning the Dijon essay prize if he took the unexpected line that the arts and sciences contribute to the *decline* of civilization, Rousseau himself was deeply convinced of the truth of what was, in Diderot's view, an obvious paradox.

In this essay Rousseau invokes Sparta, as do so many of his contemporaries, as the ideal society in which only man's basic needs are met, and in which man, rather than any artefact, represents the sum total of excellence. Sparta thus contrasts favourably with Athens, seat of luxury and refinement, of poets and orators, of painted canvas and marble statue, and therefore of vice and vain doctrine. Rousseau, as he hopefully surmised, would have made greater moral progress in Sparta, where his fellow citizens would have supplied corrective treatment for his weaknesses, than in Athens, with its atmosphere of swinish luxury. The autobiographical imperative is clearly in evidence here: if Sparta represents the lost simplicity of Geneva, then Athens is Paris, with its false values and false friendships.

Throughout Rousseau's curious argument in the Dijon prize essay runs the attractive idea of nature as moral imperative: natural man exercising his natural talents in natural surroundings for natural rewards. In Rousseau's opinion nothing could be farther from this natural condition than the essential duplicity of the work of art. This is his central theme, and he does not hesitate to give examples. These examples are dangerous, provocatively so, when the state of contemporary censorship is borne in mind. A stroll through the gardens of Versailles, says Rousseau, where corrective treatment has been applied not to man, who is in need of it, but to nature, and where one's natural progress is punctuated by statues and herms representing gods and goddesses, nymphs and satyrs, all unclothed and seductive, represents a direct challenge to man's impulse towards virtue and an invitation to join in collective corruption. For a society which can ordain such a travesty of nature must by definition be corrupt.

> Our gardens are adorned with statues and our galleries with paintings. What would you expect to be shown by these masterpieces of art, exposed to the admiration of the public? Great men who have

defended their country or those still greater who have enriched it with their virtue? No. They are images of all the aberrations of the heart and mind, carefully selected from ancient mythology and presented to the budding curiosity of our children, no doubt in order that they may have models of misconduct before their eyes before they are able to read.

It was this particular passage that struck contemporaries as a model of impassioned relevance, and the fact that it occurred in a treatise supposedly about the arts and sciences activated criticism of existing representations of "all the aberrations of the heart and mind". Boucher and his many followers could count their reputations as being compromised from the appearance in print of this essay in 1750. "As the conveniences of life are multiplied, as the arts are perfected and luxury spreads, true courage fades, the military virtues vanish, and this is the work of the sciences and all those arts which secretly exert their influence in governmental chambers."

Did Rousseau know, as he wrote those words, that the Marquis de Marigny, Mme de Pompadour's brother, destined to become Directeur des Bâtiments and thus virtual Minister of State for the Arts, was at that very moment on a tour of Italy, intended to refine his taste and prepare him for his government position? Certainly Marigny's ultimate successor, the Comte d'Angiviller, pursued a very different course, inaugurated a programme of virtuous and moral subjects to which painters and sculptors were invited to conform, kept a close watch on commissions, and seems to have been unduly sensitive to the effect of works of art on the public. In this way David's *Oath of the Horatii*, which was a royal commission, transmitted through the office of the Directeur des Bâtiments, and thus identified with state patronage, can nevertheless be linked directly with Rousseau's first discourse.

Rousseau's theory of the natural is not of course rational. It is not

even natural, for it involves the proscription of simple pleasure-giving
devices which might turn the recipient into a monster of depravity.
One such device was the theatre. Unlike many of his erstwhile
philosophe friends, Diderot, Grimm and d'Alembert, Rousseau did not
believe that the theatre performed a healthy and enlightening propaganda function as a kind of secular pulpit. He considered it, as he
considered the fine arts, as a school for perpetrating those "aberrations of the heart and mind" which afflicted his paranoid conscience.
When he learned from Diderot that there was a move afoot to establish a theatre in Geneva, his own Sparta, and that this would be given
publicity in a forthcoming article by d'Alembert for the *Encyclopédie*,
entitled "Geneva", he determined to make a reply for which he was
in fact overprepared. His *Lettre à d'Alembert sur les spectacles* (1758)
was written in three weeks and is an even more impassioned and
bewildering document than the Dijon prize essay. D'Alembert's article
is a fine piece of sophistry which suggests that Geneva would benefit
from a theatre as a school for feelings, and that the theatre would be
rewarded by Geneva with rights of citizenship for those actors and
actresss who plied their trade with virtuous intent.

It might be thought that the idea of a theatre as a disciplinary
institution would have its attractions for Rousseau, as it had for
Grimm, Diderot, and later Beaumarchais. But Rousseau contends
that for a man leading a natural life a theatre should not be necessary;
only a corrupt spirit, he says, needs frivolous amusements. The effect
of the drama is to excite the passions, and to flatter the tastes of
the audience. And axiomatically, if man is born good, as Rousseau
insists, the theatre cannot take credit for making him better. Better
than what? Argued along these lines it can be seen that a theatre is
entirely superfluous.

But of course it is more than this. It is actively dangerous. By
simulating the passions, says Rousseau, actors remind people that the
passions exist. As for comedy, even Molière is not averse to making

his effects dependent on the natural credulity or simplicity of an Orgon, an Alceste, or a Georges Dandin. To Rousseau, comedy simply provides a situation in which virtue can be subverted. Too much attention is paid to women and young lovers, not enough to the serious and the elderly. Wives and husbands neglect their duties; servants forget their place. Rousseau's natural man is so fragile, so in need of the moral guide or tutor with which he will be provided in *Émile*, that he need only witness a tender scene to be put in imminent danger of succumbing to his senses. If one is on the point of falling in love, says Rousseau, one needs inoculation, not a performance of *Zaïre*.

For the languid inhabitants of Paris, a city without industry, the boredom of inaction demands release in the unnatural atmosphere of a theatre. But the laborious and frugal citizens of a small community in Neuchâtel will live a life of natural toil that leaves no time or space for artificial entertainment. Rousseau remembers just such a township that he saw as a child, a predictably enchanted place whose inhabitants could turn out anything from a tapestry to a barometer with their bare hands. Would one impose on these enviable folk a paid spectacle that could only devalue them?

Having expended on the notion that a theatre is harmful more arguments than it could ever possibly sustain, Rousseau eases his way out of his address with a generous wave of patronage which breaks the boundaries of common sense and soars into a vision of the future which did in fact come to be realized. It is as if the whole frenetic piece of writing had been undertaken for this one moment of incantation, in which he severs any links he may once have had with the *philosophes* and brings himself to the attention of Mirabeau. If the people want entertainment, he says, let them have festivals in the open air, in which all are natural participants. Reverting once again to his unrealistically remembered childhood and youth, Rousseau attempts to make them present for everyone:

> In the midst of the pomp of great nations and their
> dreary magnificence, a secret voice must cry from
> the depths of the soul, "Ah! Where are the games
> and festivals of my youth? Where is the concord
> of the citizens? Where is brotherly love? Where are
> pure joy and true joyousness? Where are peace,
> liberty, equality, innocence? Shall we go in search of
> them again?"

He foresees a re-enactment of a celebration described by Plutarch,
in which a detachment of old men, singing of their former glory, is
succeeded by men in the prime of life, with a squad of children bring-
ing up the rear and signifying hope for the future. There can be little
doubt that this passage was to have a profound effect on David in his
orchestration of the festivals of the Revolution.

An acquaintance with these writings, with their polemical intent,
may prepare the ground for a reading of Rousseau's plans for society
in *Du contrat social*. The main premises of his thought are already
explicit: the conviction that man is intrinsically good, together with
the knowledge that he is always in danger of being corrupted; the
fear of other men's decrees, together with the desire to belong to a
virtuous and Spartan republic; the irrational arguments somehow
touching on the right note of corrective suggestion. Two short
excerpts from the *Confessions*, both of them undeniably sincere, will
underline these contradictions. In Book 2 he says:

> Modestly I imagined myself one of a narrow but
> exquisitely chosen clan, one in which I felt confident
> that I should rule. A single castle was the limit of my
> ambition. To be the friend of its lord and lady, the
> lover of their daughter, the friend of their son and
> protector of their neighbours: that would be enough;
> I required no more.

Here we see him desiring total, feudal, familial integration. But in Book 4 he says something rather more revealing:

> I passed through Geneva without going to see anyone, but I felt faint as I crossed the bridge. Never have I seen the walls of that happy city without feeling a certain disturbance of the heart, the product of an excess of emotion. The noble ideal of liberty exalted my spirit, while at the same time the thought of equality, unity, and gentleness of manners moved me to tears and inspired in me a keen regret that I had lost all these blessings. How wrong I was and yet how natural was my mistake! I imagined that I saw all this in my native land because I carried it in my own heart.

Here is a vision of the ideal republic – it would have to be a republic – based on a selective view of memory. The two excerpts would at first sight appear to be at odds; the task of *Du contrat social* is to create a structure as close as the ideal republic which will nevertheless allow its citizens to feel as fully integrated into it as they would in a family, a marriage, or a friendship.

The facts of Rousseau's life are contributory evidence. His mother died at his birth, and his father, a watchmaker, decamped to Nyon when the boy was ten years old, leaving him to be brought up by an aunt. He therefore had poor experience of family life. He was sent away to school (he had only three years' formal education) and then apprenticed to an engraver. He had little or no conception of belonging. One Sunday he was amusing himself outside the city gates, and, forgetting the lateness of the hour, found himself locked out for the night; with a feeling of sublime relief he simply walked away into Savoy. He therefore had no country, and in later life Geneva had reality only as a memory. In Savoy he fell in with a coterie of Catholics who were looking for young converts; as they promised food, shelter and affection Rousseau changed his religion. He became the ward, and later the lover, of Mme de Warens, who received a subsidy from the King of Savoy for her good work in encouraging conversions. She sent Rousseau to a seminary in Turin, which he hated.

Also in Turin he entered a noblewoman's house as a secretary, that is to say, a servant, and while there stole a pink and silver ribbon which he wanted to give to a fellow servant called Marion. He was discovered, he panicked, and he blamed the theft on that same Marion. This episode imbued him with a sense of moral worthlessness – it was compounded by certain exhibitionist tendencies to which he also confesses – and these factors convinced him that without a guiding hand he would fall into even greater depths. Mme de Warens, to whose house in Annecy he returned after a period of unemployment, had the idea of giving him a music master, and Rousseau's official occupation for the rest of his life was as a music copyist, occasional composer, and author of articles on music for the *Encyclopédie*. When Mme de Warens was about her proselytizing business, Rousseau consented to try for a job in Lyon or Lausanne or Berne or Paris. It was in Paris that he was admitted to the circle of the influential Mme Dupin, whose other visitors included Diderot, d'Alembert, and Mably. Mme Dupin procured for him a post as secretary to the French ambassador in Venice; predictably this was a disaster, for Rousseau was never to become attuned to taking orders. He showed an alarming tendency to walk away, and an amazing complacency about living in other people's houses.

After a year in Venice he returned to Paris and devoted himself to his music. After the Dijon prize essay was published in 1750 his little opera, *Le Devin du village*, was performed at court. The King offered him a pension, but owing to various social embarrassments that afflicted him Rousseau could not pluck up the courage to go and collect it. It was not fear of the King that stopped him, he tells us; it was fear of the contempt of the lackeys. As is all too well known, he married a laundrymaid, had five children, and put them all into a foundling home. Like his father, he expressed no desire ever to see them again.

He was dramatically ill for most of his life, and as no doctor could cure him he insisted on a post-mortem. This showed him to be physically sound, but of course dead. In a sense he was a psychosomatic theorist, because what he experienced as a malaise he interpreted as a malaise in society. He thus formed a habit of projecting his own needs on to a larger entity, or translating those needs as societal requirements. His *Confessions* spell out for us his extreme morbidity. He was paranoid, hypochondriacal, and above all guilty. Certain physical ailments gave him a sense of lasting shame which threw him at times into fits of madness, and which certainly account for his endless and restless wanderings. His habitual state was worthlessness: hence, "I want to be what I should be." At the same time he is an enduring and inspiring moralist. This conflict should be borne in mind when considering the startling propositions enshrined in his Social Contract.

Rousseau's strong suit consists of flinging down the gauntlet. Thus Part II of the *Discourse on Inequality* begins with the words, "The first man who, having enclosed a piece of land, took it into his head to say, 'This is mine,' and found people simple enough to believe him, was the true founder of civil society." This proposition, not that property is theft, but that property is vice, was an unbelievable audacity in the Paris of the 1750s and 1760s. It is tempered (in 1754) by some extremely academic argument about the difference between despotism and paternal authority, just as the main argument of *Du contrat social* has been relinquished in favour of its opening proposition, possibly the most famous sentence penned in the eighteenth century and never allowed to slip into disuse from that day to this.

Du contrat social begins with the words, "Man is born free and everywhere he is in chains." These chains are the corrupt and corrupting institutions of the eighteenth-century state. How to remedy this situation? Quite simple. Both men and institutions must be remade and re-educated in order to provide the maximum guarantee of integration and protection the one for the other. They must enter into a covenant – a contract or pact – by which both will benefit.

This will be done firstly by drawing a distinction between freedom and liberty. Freedom is a dangerous individual prerogative which allows men to steal, rape, plunder and kill, in order to satisfy their individual desires. By that definition, free men cannot live together in society. But liberty is a civic condition, whereby the individual surrenders to the state his selfish freedom, in exchange for protection from the selfish freedoms of others. Since all have to gain from this exchange they will entrust their liberty to each other, or to an impersonal necessity known as the General Will, *le moi commun* as against *le moi humain*. Only decrees agreed to by all will have the force of the General Will. Any sectarian or splinter groups will represent the Particular Will, or *moi humain*, and it is the task of the citizens to discipline and enlighten deviants who still hold the Particular Will, so that they may remember the overriding needs of their fellow citizens, and thus surrender their residual freedom to the greater ideal of Liberty. This is the Social Contract.

Who is to enforce this ideal state of affairs? Everybody, it seems. Men, being honourable and sensible creatures, will see that the good of each is tantamount to the good of all, for as each is subsumed in all, the greater number will take care of the individual. And, by implication, the danger of individual wrongdoing is, or will be, removed for ever by the vigilance of that loving, judging, protecting totality.

But how is this community to be governed? Here Rousseau falls into the casuistry that has done so much damage to the modern state. The people is sovereign because it embodies the General Will. But there is a character called the Legislator, or Lawgiver, who symbolizes the General Will, and whose task it is to reveal to the public what it really wants.

> Individuals see the good and reject it; the public
> desires the good but does not see it. Both equally need
> guidance. Individuals must be obliged to subordinate
> their will to their reason; the public must be taught to
> recognize what it desires. Such public enlightenment
> would produce a measure of understanding, and will,
> in the social body, bring the parts into perfect
> harmony and lift the whole to its fullest strength.
> Hence the necessity of a lawgiver.

The only way that Rousseau can get around the anomaly of having a Lawgiver, when it is acknowledged that the General Will is law, is to give him no power at all: he is pure Mind. There is an echo here of his "I want to be what I should be." With the Lawgiver he is postulating the necessity of a General Conscience.

Complications set in. The execution of the laws in this political system is entrusted to a *government*.

> What then is a government? An intermediary body
> established between the subjects and the sovereign
> for their mutual communication, a body charged
> with the execution of the laws and the maintenance
> of freedom, both civil and political. The members of
> this body are called magistrates or kings, that is to
> say governors, and the whole body bears the name
> of prince.

It is at this point that we discover with some surprise that Rousseau's ideal state is a hierarchical structure. Although a citizen of Geneva, he cannot divest himself of the French notion of a sovereign. We can accept the existence of a Lawgiver, that pure creature whose function, as Rousseau says, is to *persuade* men to be what they should be, but when Rousseau proposes a sovereign government, whose hypothetical function is to translate the General Will into laws, his argument loses its original clarity, and words lose their original meaning. It is no longer clear whether "sovereign" means the body politic or the prince. Therefore it is necessary for him to propose another Social Contract, between the people and the prince.

> . . . the dominant will of the prince is or ought to be only the General Will or the law, and his force nothing other than the public force concentrated in his hands; as soon as he resolves to perform on his own authority some absolute and independent act, the union of all begins to slacken. And if in the end it comes about that the prince has a particular will more active than that of the sovereign, and if in order to enforce obedience to this particular will he uses the public force which is in his hands, with the result that there are so to speak two sovereigns, one *de jure* and one *de facto*, then the social bond dissolves at once and the body politic is dissolved.

Rousseau still maintains that the Lawgiver is there to act as referee or umpire. For he is aware that the particular will acts unceasingly against the General Will, which is still the visionary desideratum. He argues that the solution to this dilemma is a democratic monarchy, such as obtains in England, although it is not clear whether or not he believes that the English monarch is elected. This is one of those theories that work on paper. Suffrage is universal.

It is clear that constitutional practice matters less to Rousseau than the central preoccupation of the entire document: how man may be corrected, turned into a good citizen, and made to be what he should be by submitting to the General Will, which means having his particular dissenting voice silenced by the contemplation of the good of all, and by turning *le moi humain* into *le moi commun*. It may by now seem that the original man who was born free has become fettered even more securely by Rousseau's discipline than by any other, and the pattern has been widely embraced by totalitarian regimes of both left and right. But if this is now a dangerous and Machiavellian creed, it must be remembered that Rousseau belongs to a generation which believed firmly in the perfectibility of man. Rousseau's aim is not to make men free, as in the ferocious dawn of time, but to make them social beings. This is indeed an ideal undertaking, and it has the hallmarks of virtue, which, it was held, all men possess.

For Winckelmann and his followers, perfect man was man at the beginning of history; for Diderot and Rousseau and Voltaire perfect man is what will be found at the other end of the historical process, when truth will prevail and men will be honourable and loving and courteous and desirous of the good of others. This ideal has been eclipsed many times, yet there are few who would not subscribe to it.

As states go, Rousseau's turns out to be rather cumbersome, and rather rigidly structured. There is the main mass of the citizens arguing each other into complying with the General Will, and being persuaded to keep up the good work by the Legislator or Lawgiver. There is the Prince or Sovereign who rules them but who can be deposed if he does not comply with the General Will of the citizens. And to keep him in line there is a Magistrate to see that the Social Contract is observed among all parties. He obeys a body called the Tribunate, which, says Rousseau, is guardian of the laws and of the legislative power. Members of the Tribunate must have an even more developed super-ego than the other parties to the contract, because although they answer to no-one and have no executive or legislative powers, they have a right of veto, which is apparently absolute. And to prevent their gaining too much power they can be suspended at will and by law – but Rousseau does not say by whom. And if those who uphold the General Will are not satisfied that it is being obeyed, a temporary dictator can be appointed, as in ancient Rome.

The species of upward mobility required by an enterprising individual desirous of controlling everything was of course demonstrated by Napoleon, although in no other single respect does France during the Revolution and Empire resemble Rousseau's state. The fact that Napoleon claimed that Rousseau was responsible for the Revolution of 1789 is probably no more than evidence of his own reading. But it is significant that when the Senate was trying to enforce Napoleon's abdication in 1814 one of the charges against him was that he had broken the Social Contract.

All that remains to be discussed is the matter of a state religion. And here Rousseau draws a sharp distinction between the religion of the private man, which is a silent, meditative, quietist affair, and the religion of the citizen, which has dogmas and rituals laid down by law, and which enjoins men to worship both God and the law. Reference need hardly be made here to Robespierre's cult of the Supreme Being, or the Festivals of the Revolution, which played on such a combination of associations. These too were corrective entertainments, certain of which opened with a salvo of artillery to summon the citizens to their observances.

Rousseau's document ends with a confession, characteristically, that he should have examined matters such as foreign policy, but that he has not done so because foreign policy might be outside his range. He has been outside his range in several chapters, but he has always returned to his central argument: that the main crime of the citizen is to be anti-social (as he was himself). It should be remembered that this essay, the most influential of all eighteenth-century Utopian exercises, sprang from a deep need to be wanted and essential and useful and good – all matters which proved, as he would say, to be outside his range.

It should also be remembered that having propounded this ideal of liberty Rousseau chose freedom. As a boy, nightfall had surprised him outside the city gates of Geneva, and released him from *le moi commun* to *le moi humain*. Later in his life his wanderings became a matter of necessity rather than of choice. In 1762 he went from Paris to Yverdon to Môtiers; in 1765 from the Île de Saint-Pierre to Basel to England. He subsisted for the rest of his life in the paradoxical position of doing what he wanted to do at the expense of private patrons, and there is evidence that he was aware of the incongruity. The mental breakdown of 1776, when he tried to distribute copies of the *Confessions* in the streets of Paris, after having failed to place them on the High Altar of Notre Dame, testifies to his failure to achieve a place in the ideal institution, an institution based on the voluntary alienation of certain rights in order to obtain, in exchange, certain privileges. In writing *Du contrat social* Rousseau was operating as a free man, but a free man longing for civil liberty, for protection as well as for discipline. Although the strain may have proved too great, at least for Rousseau himself, it is surely significant that "liberty" becomes such a crucial word in the social engineering of the Revolution.

The Revolution, however, was not yet in sight. What unites Rousseau with the Neoclassicists is the belief in certain perfect forms; what makes Rousseau so singular is his almost clinical need for perfect behaviour, or for the belief that in certain conditions perfect behaviour will be possible. The weakness of *Du contrat social* springs from the almost impossible task of trying to create a reality which could contain, must contain, the ideal. Winckelmann set himself an easier task when he claimed that the ideal had existed in the past and could be recaptured by imitation. But Winckelmann is a static thinker. He recognizes only a physical imperative, albeit one which incorporates certain moral values. In Rousseau the real and the ideal are confused in the most burdensome, the most painful way. For in a state of liberty man both desires and abominates a structure, desires it because it guarantees him the necessities of life, and abominates it because it denies him freedom. Rousseau invented the General Will much as Jung was to invent the Collective Unconscious, and both men were probably animated by the same desire: the desire to find a unifying answer to the confusion of reality. In the eighteenth century only Diderot, rising effortlessly on the contemporary wave, with his belief in the future kept buoyant but practicable, was able to live existentially. And even Diderot died foretelling an era of bloodshed, as if divine optimism were a gift that had to be surrendered in the fullness of time.

In the *Rêveries d'un promeneur solitaire* Rousseau pinpoints for us the manner in which *Du contrat social* has become subject to distortion. "My temperament has had a great influence on my maxims, or rather my habits; for I have never behaved according to the rules, or rather I have never followed any rules other than those prompted by my nature." But Rousseau was aware that it was in fact his nature that required corrective treatment. He is both a nostalgic and wilful solitary – hence his understanding of freedom – and a rigorous logician – hence his concept of liberty. He has a Cornelian ideal of virtue, which is essentially the ability to triumph over the passions, and an eighteenth-century belief in a reconstructed society. In his interesting *Lettre à Voltaire sur la providence*, an answer to Voltaire's poem on the Lisbon earthquake, he states, "I believe in God . . . because doubt is too violent a state for me to endure." This statement sheds additional light on the impersonal impetus behind *Du contrat social*. In every other respect it is of its time: in its belief in the future, its desire for the good, its general optimism. These imponderables are still valid. It is the history of the twentieth century that makes them seem so intangible.

5

The Rhetoric of Sensations*

"*Q̲UEL TRISTE ET PLAT métier que celui de critique,*" wrote Diderot for the benefit of his august but unseen public in 1763. Two years later, in a letter to Sophie Volland, he congratulates himself on the success and pleasure which his task has brought him: "*il m'amuse moi-même*". In the first volume of this new edition of the *Salons*, fruit of a seamless collaboration between Jean Seznec and Jean Adhémar, now in an attractive smaller format, we can follow him from his uneasy undistinguished début to the point at which his immense and underestimated craftsmanship enables him to dominate with almost physical ease a medium designed for hacks.

The difference between the rachitic *Salon* of 1759 – his first – and the torrential and stupefying *Salon* of 1767 can be foreseen, albeit tentatively, in this first volume, which takes us up to 1763. The characteristics of Diderot's maturity, the impertinence and enthusiasm, are here already; unfortunately they fail to produce a single opinion of any value, apart from his reverence for Chardin, which was widely shared by Chardin's contemporaries. No matter; reality, for Diderot, began when he threw away the catalogue, disregarded the artist's intentions, and concentrated on his own reactions not only to what was but to what might have been. His doting editor, Grimm, mindful of the need to keep his subscribers amused, let him rip. Written in

*Diderot: *Salons*. Volume I: 1759 1761 1763. Edited by Jean Seznec and Jean Adhémar. Clarendon Press. *The Times Literary Supplement*, 3 October 1975.

circumstances which would only make sense to us if the whole of
French painting between 1759 and 1781 were to be destroyed, the Salons
covered by this volume did not burden Diderot with too much gravity.
It is therefore essential to follow through, for on the showing of these
early years a suspicion begins to creep in that he plays the part of court
jester a little too willingly and that his task is eased by the unsatisfactory mixture of timidity and licence which characterized French
painting in the 1760s.

The interest of the further volumes lies in the way in which
Diderot's sunny gifts of expostulation and of rapture are gradually
nudged towards something like sobriety by the immense change of
style that was to spread across Europe from Rome and was
posthumously to be christened Neoclassicism.

Diderot considered that his main qualification for pronouncing on
the arts of painting, sculpture and engraving was his understanding
of the passions. Yet what he called passions we would recognize
merely as the rhetoric of sensations. There is nothing painful, bitter,
or unresolved here, none of the loyalty that transcends error that we
find in Baudelaire or the fearlessness that characterizes Zola. Even less
is there the tranquillizing serenity of the non-aligned for which we
read Fromentin. For passion, in the eighteenth-century understanding
of the word, presents itself as an eminently agreeable state, a sort of
hectic vitality which gives one full licence to change one's mien, stance
and opinion fifty times within the hour. People thus enabled to go
skidding along the paths traced out by their senses – and Diderot is the
supreme example – did not get on terribly well with those in the grip
of an *idée fixe*. It is surely no accident that Diderot fell out with his
three closest friends: J.J. Rousseau (described as *"méchant"* because he
did not like Paris), J.B. Greuze (*"Je n'aime plus Greuze"*), and the sculptor Falconet, the only man of the entire century to give Diderot his
comeuppance by closing the door in his face. The fact that Rousseau,
Greuze and Falconet were probably unbearable to be with is, for the

moment, irrelevant. What is to be retained is the fact that as a critic Diderot is also a tyrant, at least until 1767, when the permissiveness of the age that formed him begins to crumble before a new ideology. To disagree with Diderot was to be axed; even Grimm's editorial interpolations are mollifying and indulgent. In these early *Salons* we see the outline of Diderot's genius taking shape; it is the genius of the infant prodigy or the spoilt child, and it will only be rendered durable by a consummate literary skill and by unexpectedly weighty opposition.

For the moment, i.e. until 1763, there are no problems. Most French painting is mediocre but could be improved if Diderot were to be consulted. Dominated at one end of the scale by the pompous and unloved Pierre and at the other by Boucher, the balance is maintained by Chardin, Old Master of a time and country which had no mind to produce such figures. For the armchair traveller there is Vernet, describing very beautifully and in great detail the ports of France or lashing up a storm at sea to remind us of the dominance of nature. For the armchair psychologist there is Greuze, star of the Salon of 1761, with his sulkily pretty account of a village betrothal which had Diderot and his public offering an amazing wealth of opinion on qualities of "expression". The obligatory bulk of religious paintings is roughly handled, for a good reason (they are not particularly interesting) and for a bad one (Christianity is not an attractive mythology). We can breeze by the subtle painful portraits of Perronneau; they happen to be the works of an obstinate and private individual. We learn a lot about the mediocrity of Challe and the genius of Deshays (both now equally forgotten); we ponder the sobriety and *bon goût* of Vien but doubt his wisdom in choosing to paint subjects more suitable to the medium of bas-relief. There is evidence that Chardin tried to put in a restraining word here and there; it was recorded but not retained. At first with stealth, then with the impatience of a man outstripping his medium, Diderot discards whatever disciplines good taste and decorum originally imposed on him. And by 1763 he has the exuberance born of the knowledge that he can out-talk anybody, anywhere, particularly if he is determined to dominate the conversation in the first place.

Enter now, on a far distant horizon, Johann Joachim Winckelmann, dithyrambic librarian from Dresden, by this time happily translated to Rome. After a longer and harder apprenticeship than that served by Diderot, Winckelmann achieved European fame in 1763 with his *Geschichte der Kunst des Altertums*, a treatise on the art of the Ancients which was, interestingly enough, as devoid of illustrations as were Diderot's *Salons*. The lacunae in Winckelmann's knowledge of Greek and Roman art were immense, but irrelevant to his theme and also to his style: he seemed to know and understand a limited aspect of the ancient world far better than any scholar had ever done before.

Winckelmann's ring of confidence is based on simple assertion: perfect beauty, which is characterized by noble simplicity and calm grandeur, is to be found in the art of the Ancients, and those modern artists who wish to become perfect should either proceed in an ancient manner (disdaining passion and extravagant gesture, distilling a generalized beauty – *beau idéal* – from a range of individual examples) or indeed should copy the subject-matter and gestures of classical statuary.

This simple recommendation was to provide an aesthetic creed for a century which had not realized that it needed one. Words like "grandeur", "severity", "simplicity", and "perfection", with their reproving and uplifting undertones, put an effective stop to the restlessness of experimentation, rather as an injection of morphine will immobilize an agitated patient. The theory was accepted with rapture as it spread from Rome to France and England, where civil servants and country squires were preparing to grace their station in life by improving their taste. The curious minimalism of much of Neoclassical art, as well as its occasional sublimities, developed quite independently of Winckelmann, for whom the sight of the Apollo Belvedere or the Laocoön were nothing less than glimpses of a finer world, one which had once existed and had now vanished like the Garden of Eden.

In this paradise the climate was mild all the year round (Winckelmann never went to Greece), the arts of civility were practised, and physical perfection was universal. The book was translated into French in 1766 and was to be unchallenged for the better part of a century. It was left to Jean-Jacques Rousseau to point out that if those comely youths could afford to spend so much time oiling up for the arena it was only because the economies of Athens and Sparta operated on a basis of slave labour. He has never got the credit he deserves for this observation, Winckelmann's theories proving more eerily powerful.

While travellers to and from Rome were rhapsodizing over the theory of the imitation of the Ancients, as it was then called, Diderot was still at his desk in Paris, and, despite his perpetual good humour, feeling somewhat left out. For Diderot, who had a proprietorial interest in the future of French painting, and who reserved to himself the monopoly of improving it, this new standard of excellence imported from abroad was something of an irritant. Moreover, as a philosopher, or even just as a Frenchman, he grasped the logical absurdity of it: the examples of the past must of necessity preclude further invention, and the imitation of an accepted norm could admit few variables.

An art without variables, without the volatility that made it quite literally always different, admitting the free flow of sensation and reaction, was so repellent a prospect to Diderot that it roused him to his moment of true passion as a critic. In the *Salon* of 1767 there is an extraordinary, and extraordinarily angry, incantation, a series of sentences beginning with the words *"Modèle idéal, ligne vraie"*, in which Diderot provides his own theory of the ideal model. And his own model is man's endless groping towards perfectibility, the mental vision he has of what should be rather than what has been. It is not something acquired by copying. It is the property of a genius who sees how elements of the natural world can be perfected. Ironically this *Salon*, like all the others, was never published in Diderot's lifetime, and this alternative theory was known only to Diderot's friends and associates. The weakness of Winckelmann's ideas is demonstrated by the fact that Neoclassicism could only develop by a process of lateral thinking. The strength of Diderot's vision was ratified by every new thought and change of style. Confusion is further compounded by the fact that historians of eighteenth-century art are liable to collide when they evaluate the art of Jacques-Louis David, who put into practice the theories of either Winckelmann or Diderot, depending on which theory is currently in favour.

But Winckelmann's *Geschichte* proved to be formative in the career of Diderot the art critic. After 1767 the rudeness and the self-indulgence diminish. A more than defensive desire for vindication is evident, and pictures which had previously amused or titillated are now dismissed as unworthy. Diderot had invested much in Greuze, whose family tragedies seemed to promise deep emotion. Yet in 1769, when Greuze made a bid for academic honours with his picture *Severus and Caracalla*, a picture which he claimed to be based on Poussin (always an honorary Ancient in French eyes), Diderot was merely exasperated. He considered it pretentious copying; hence *"Je n'aime plus Greuze."* And his own desires became more compelling, his need to extol the varieties and beauties of the world more urgent. And since there is a limit to the number of times one can make the same point, Diderot's stylistic brilliance makes his case for him. Descriptions are interspersed with digressions, dialogues, ekphrases, rhapsodies, even dreams. No matter if the artist is still Vernet or Chardin; their works are merely illustrations of the variability, or what he would call, with no trace of fear, the "vicissitudes" of life. And when the Messianic painter, David, does come, in 1781, Diderot will simply comment, in recognition or exhaustion, *"Il a de l'âme."*

The split between Winckelmann and Diderot, between the theorist chasing too few ideas and the existential experimenter, is important. It will be reiterated with less clarity in the new war between the Ancients and the Moderns which will be subsumed under the heading of the Romantic Movement. The eighteenth century abounds in authoritarians proclaiming the one true way to perfection, and presenting beguiling structures based almost entirely on words. The importance of Diderot, who is no less monopolistic than Winckelmann or Rousseau, lies in his loyalty to his own life, times and standards. To the current fashionable preoccupation with a past which could somehow be magically recreated, Diderot administers a corrective: the object lesson of a life without cerebral nostalgia. Through the medium of describing pictures in words he establishes an alternative to cults, programmes, systems and aesthetic syllabuses, and with a persistent note of remedial anarchy he reminds us that it is an error not to enjoy a world as tangible as a peach painted by Chardin.

His influence on the art of his time was probably not very great, certainly far less important that that of Winckelmann. Yet this was never a very relevant issue, for Diderot had no consistent programme for himself or for others. What he did have, paradoxically enough, was his own *modèle idéal*, the philosopher whom he decribes as Ariste in a fragment written in 1758 and incorporated into the *Essai sur la poésie dramatique*. *"On l'avait surnommé le philosophe, parce qu'il était né sans ambition, qu'il avait l'âme honnête, et que l'envie n'en avait jamais altéré la douceur et la paix. Du reste, grave dans son maintien, sévère dans ses moeurs, austère et simple dans ses discours, le manteau d'un ancien philosophe était presque la seule chose qui lui manquait; car il était pauvre et content de sa pauvreté."* Diderot assumed that all his friends would recognize him from this description, which remains grotesquely inaccurate to this day. It is true that the rude and ebullient performer of 1763 became a graver man. But Diderot was never an Ancient: he was pre-eminently modern. He even earned his living in a modern way. And Winckelmann's system would, he thought, soon be out of date.

(This was incorect.) Diderot, of course, had no system at all, and this is his achievement. From a *"triste et plat métier"* he fashioned a profession which could speak with any voice. It is we, his successors, who are in graver need of a *modèle idéal*.

6

The Observer Obliviated*

THE THEME OF THIS dramatic book is so novel and at the same time so nebulous that one reads the text with mounting anxiety in case the argument, which purports to be cumulative, should escape one altogether. It is not only necessary but essential to state this argument at the outset, to let one's immediate reactions disperse, and to haul one's most dispassionate critical apparatus into position.

This process will not be accomplished without a sigh of something more than effort, for Michael Fried involves one in a lot of hard work; at the same time he manages to convey the information that hard work is his particular province, and that "modern scholars" or "modern commentators", whom he arraigns on numerous occasions throughout the text, simply repeat each other's clichés.

The argument can be stated as follows. In France, in the middle of the eighteenth century, a determined and conscious effort was made by the painter to seek a new relationship with the spectator or beholder of his picture. This was to be achieved by certain stratagems, the function of which was to re-establish the "ontological status" or autonomy of the picture itself.

For this reason it would be necessary to deny the spectator or beholder access to the picture, and this could be achieved by letting the characters depicted interact with one another across the picture

*Absorption and Theatricality: Painting and Beholder in the Age of Diderot by Michael Fried. University of California Press. *The Times Literary Supplement*, 3 April 1981.

plane to the exclusion of any possible audience. In order to "obliviate" the spectator it might be necessary for the painter to depict personages with their backs to him or lost in self-absorption or facing each other and behaving or performing in apparent unconsciousness that they are being regarded.

The effect on the spectator, who had of course been there all along, would be to titillate his curiosity – which would be curiosity mixed with a certain pique or voyeurism – and the spectator so ignored would thus be teased into looking harder at something that purported to be getting on very well without him. The characters depicted in activities such as drawing, sleeping, reading, conversing, etc. would be participating in an "absorptive" mode of being which would not only establish their own primacy but would place the spectator in a subordinate relation to the painter and to the thing painted.

It is stated that this process was started by Chardin, who on two occasions depicted a draughtsman, with his back to the spectator, sketching Pigalle's *Mercury*, and that it was perfected by Greuze who, by painting multi-figure dramas of great emotional complexity and heightened plotting, managed to "screen the audience out" or at least "refuse to allow the fact of its existence to impinge on the absorbed consciousness of its figures". So, it is argued, instead of appealing to an audience, as most traditional criticism of this painter would seem to establish, the paintings of Greuze do in fact neutralize the very presence of an audience by allowing it no function in the perception of the pictures, and thereby inviting it to react, presumably in a mood of fascinated frustration, to the "absorptive" modes thus shown, and shown to be so strong that they exclude or "obliviate" the spectator or beholder.

It is then argued that David, observing that Greuze had perfected this method, had to have recourse to more extreme stratagems, and proposed one in *Belisarius Receiving Alms* by introducing into the picture a surrogate spectator (the soldier with his arms raised in disbelief), by swivelling round the viewpoint so that Belisarius faces across the canvas instead of out of it, and by opening up the back of the picture space by a series of perspectival devices so as actively to repel the spectator or even as it were to send him off to ricochet against the opposite wall.

The spectator, thus teased, negated, "obliviated", and physically sent packing, is not however altogether denied access to the picture space. He can, for example, look at landscapes, into which artists will positively invite his participation by placing clumps of figures, engaged in different activities, at different levels of depth in the imagined space. The spectator can thus enter this space; indeed this is sanctioned by Diderot who, in the *Salon* of 1767, describes the landscapes of Joseph Vernet as a sequence of imaginary promenades taken in the company of an imaginary *abbé*. By his permitted and imaginary wanderings in this confected and imaginary landscape the spectator is not only allowed an extreme measure of "existential reverie" but is "removed" from in front of the picture.

Since this method is sanctioned by Diderot (but I think only for Diderot himself) it is necessary to review certain pronouncements by this writer which devolve upon the "supreme fiction", i.e. that the beholder does not exist. This supreme fiction will best be served by representations of "absorptive" activities, ranging from sleeping and reading to more complicated depictions of action and passion, served up in a dramatic "tableau" (Professor Fried prefers this word to picture) of the type perfected by Greuze. "Physical entry" and thus removal from the traditional viewpoint will correspond with the pastoral mode of painting. Thus in two different ways the spectator will be displaced from his time-honoured position with regard to both the dramatic and the pastoral representations of subject-matter, the two modes of painting which, Fried says, predominated in eighteenth-century France.

Several caveats can be entered at this stage, the most obvious being an objection to the idea of the "supreme fiction", namely that the spectator is not there. A fiction even more supreme, surely, is that the painter does not require the comprehension of the spectator – a fiction indeed, particularly in pictures such as Greuze's *Fils puni*, one of Fried's examples, in which the spectator's empathy is essential to complete the import of the passions or actions depicted. Secondly it can be argued that Diderot's recommendations that the spectator be "obliviated" are spasmodic and can be directly contradicted by other passages in his writings which establish the centrality of the spectator to the whole enterprise, and of which the most celebrated example is contained in the *Essai sur la peinture* of 1756: "*Touche-moi, étonne-moi, fais-moi tressaillir, pleurer, frémir, m'indigner d'abord; tu récréeras mes yeux après, si tu veux.*"

Thirdly it can argued that Diderot's most explicit requirement, that of the surrogate spectator (which he discerned is an engraving after a supposed Van Dyck Belisarius subject) is contained in a letter to Sophie Volland which no one else could have read and which was thus not common artistic currency at the time. Fourthly it can be argued that any painter who seeks to "obliviate" the spectator should ask himself why he is exhibiting his paintings, or, in the case of Greuze, charging him an entrance fee for the obliviating experience of looking at them more carefully in the privacy of the artist's studio. Fifthly it can be argued that the *apparent* exclusion of the spectator did not suddenly erupt in France in 1750 but was long established in European art. It is in fact the precondition of every *Sacra Conversazione* where it is assumed that the spectator exists in the terrestrial world and the beings depicted are in Paradise, so that although the spectator is allowed a glimpse of the Madonna and Child and Saints he is precluded from their company by the fact that he is still living and still unregenerate.

It could further be objected that not many painters in eighteenth-century France would have immediately understood what Fried is talking about. How many of them, for example, would have been at home with the following statements?

> At the same time, taking Diderot's writings as the definitive formulation of a conception of painting that *up to a point was widely shared* [my italics], it was only by negating the beholder's presence that this could be achieved: only by establishing the fiction of his absence or non-existence could his actual placement before and enthralment by the painting be secured. This paradox directs attention to the problematic character not only of the painter–beholder relationship but of something still more fundamental – the *object*–beholder (one is tempted to say object–"subject") relationship which the painter–beholder relationship epitomizes. In Diderot's writings on painting and drama the object–beholder relationship as such, the very condition of spectatordom, stands indicted as theatrical, a medium of transcendence; and the success of both arts, in fact their continued functioning as major expressions of the human spirit, are held to depend upon whether or not painter and dramatist are able to undo their state of affairs, to *detheatricalize beholding* and so make it once again a mode of access to truth and conviction, albeit a truth and conviction that cannot be entirely equated with any known or experienced before.

I take this to mean that the spectator is not to plant himself in front of the canvas, expecting to enjoy the picture, but is to be arrested by the apparent indifference of the characters, actions and passions depicted to whether he is there, enjoying himself, or not. What is far from clear, and moreover can never be established, is the character of the perception of this archetypal eighteenth-century spectator, whether he reacted in a markedly novel manner to what purports to be a markedly novel stratagem, or, as I suspect, he took it all for granted, knowing, with every bit of commonsense that he possessed, that in a two-dimensional representation of anything he was in all instances being manipulated into an appropriate state of visual and psychological receptivity.

It will not do to take Diderot as the average spectator; Diderot is too speculative, too volatile, too interfering, too clever a journalist to bear consistently any of the constructs which Fried lays upon him. It would have provided a useful appendix to have aligned all the multiform internal contradictions in Diderot's writings on art, or to analyse his intellectual dependence on the fictive dialogue in which he arranges contrasting arguments, and in which his opponent often proves the more successful. Diderot is more like Rameau's Nephew than Fried will allow him to be. "Surrogates in Diderot's criticism" would prove to be as fertile a subject as Fried's last chapter, in which he proposes the altogether more straightforward fiction of the surrogate spectator in various representations of the Belisarius theme.

If, as it seems to me, Fried is talking about modes of perception, he is arguing from the wrong premises. To propose the examples of pictures which purport to alienate the spectator (or to "obliviate" him) while ignoring, in that same artist's work, pictures which solicit his attention – and numerous examples can be found in the work of Chardin, Greuze and David – is not, as Fried would say, to clinch the argument. To browse, with almost Proustian sensibility, on states of attention which have little to do with the abrupt and rapid mood changes of Diderot, and then to attribute this sensibility to Diderot himself, is more than misleading; it is incorrect. Here is a surprisingly harmonious but intellectually worrying sentence about the landscapes by Vernet exhibited in the *Salon* of 1767 and Diderot's reaction to them:

But because these solicitations are subsumed within a
unified and immediately apprehensible decorative
scheme, the cumulative effect of their dispersal and
resistance to any resolving hegemony is one neither of
dissociation nor of discord but of what may be thought
of as deferral (of the *satisfaction* of unity) – a deferral
and a satisfaction analogous to those of Diderot's
fictive *promenades* through Vernet's paintings in the
Salon of 1767.

Professor Fried envisages the eighteenth-century artist as living in a
pure void, divorced from social, literary or political influences and
preoccupied only with his relationship with the beholder of his paintings. This may well be true, and too much may have been made of the
opposite case, which sees the painter as part of his times, acted upon
by the thought of his times, and very frequently responding to the
spirit of his times.

If the latter case is well served, it is because it contains most of the
facts that can be established, and because it is the historian's task to
establish facts, and, if possible, to interpret them. Fried has chosen a
much more difficult task, and one which no-one living today may be
able to perform, or to substantiate: he has decided to investigate
motives which are never made explicit, reactions which are never
described (such as the fragments of Diderot's theory quoted above),
ideas which may or may not have been in the public domain and
therefore consciousness, and high points of stasis which were in fact
subject to the fluctuations of the painter's own change of heart or
the solicitations of experiment.

For the painting of eighteenth-century France is various and
bewildering, concerned with native or semi-native traditions (Rococo), the impact of teachings from abroad (Neoclassicism), and the
desire of individual artists to make new syntheses out of disparate

modes. The most powerful single general movement is towards a tighter unity of the figure subject, and a desire to endow it with the moral significance that it formerly possessed in the works of Poussin. To imply, as Fried does, that painters like Greuze and David, who were dominated by the idea of significance, should try to achieve this by "obliviating" the spectator (for whom the lesson was intended) is a brave but partial undertaking. Even the criticism of Diderot, so apparently solipsistic, can be shown to have been written with the idea of participation, reified as dialogue, in mind.

It is therefore particularly speculative to build an entire case on a reaction which cannot be tested, namely the reaction of the contemporary spectator, and a motive, that of the contemporary painter, which remains undisclosed. Moreover, to make claims that this line of argument will bring one to the essential truth about mid-eighteenth-century painting in France is to manipulate the reader much as Fried proposes that the painter manipulates the beholder. It is a marvellous idea, but it remains an idea: it is not yet proven. But as Professor Fried intends to take it further (he instances the victims on Géricault's *Raft of the Medusa*, who prefer to attract the attention of the brig *Argus* rather than solicit that of the spectator), it is to be hoped that we will be given the opportunity to test the idea once more on a future occasion.

7

Propagandist of the *Pauvre Moi* *

O N I MAY 1846, Baudelaire (or Baudelaire Dufaÿs as he then called himself) flung down gauntlets in several different and contro-versial arenas. He was supposed to be reporting on the collection of paintings exhibited to the public of that year, yet, without going through the medium of the press, for his *Salon* was published as an independent brochure, he evolved a surefire formula for wooing, attacking, promoting, reinforcing and acknowledging phenomena as different as the bourgeoisie, painters of hackneyed sentimental themes, Delacroix, his own role as interpreter, and the primacy of Balzac as supreme man of letters. All this material, and much more, is compressed into a superficially reassuring shape and given unity by a tone of uncharacteristic buoyancy.

But although the form of the *Salon* is impressively unified, it becomes evident, on further readings, that the thesis as a whole is devoid of internal logic. Extremely disparate areas of argument, each cunningly contingent on the last sentence of the previous chapter (*"Le romantisme et la couleur me conduisent droit à Eugène Delacroix"*), are brought into some kind of unity by the dazzling forensic performance of the author; and the fact that these areas of argument crop up again and again in Baudelaire's prose writings persuades us either that the *Salon* is perfectly reasonable, or that we have, through some fault of

* *Baudelaire. Salon de 1846.* Texte établi et présenté par David Kelley. Clarendon Press. *The Times Literary Supplement*, 7 March 1975.

our own, missed the vital connection that would convey its point. This is, above all, superlative journalism. But we are condemned to read it as prose, and in David Kelley's learned exegesis meant to compare it with contemporary *Salons* intended as journalism. No wonder that the elastic membrane of Baudelaire's text sags from time to time beneath the weight of interpretation bearing down on it.

Did Baudelaire really possess the enormously complicated crypto-moral system here outlined as early as 1846? He was, after all, only twenty-five and given to dying his hair green. Mr Kelley argues that the divergent artistic tendencies of the 1840s imposed a considerable task on the critic. This is irrefutable, but it can also be argued that Baudelaire saw the moral crisis of the century as parameter of his own predicament, and that in 1846 he saw it only tentatively. Baudelaire possessed a sense of sin and a faith in the releasing power of naïveté, or transparency. And like any dismayed and desperate person he tended to accumulate fetishes along the way, the most potent of which was Delacroix. Having recently been cast into the financial lower depths by family decree, he was compelled to make a career as a journalist in order to support his picturesque existence as a poet. When the result-ing affluence did not materialize, his jaunty and ephemeral confidence gave way and was replaced by a sort of agony, part psychic, part physical, which impelled him to release bitterly serious accounts of his likes and dislikes, or, more properly, of his needs and desires. That these turned into some of the noblest passages ever written about works of art is due to the miraculous power of literature, his true patrimony, as much as to the uplifting power of the images he was purporting to discuss.

What distinguishes the *Salon* of 1846 from the routine *Salon* of 1845, the tragically incomplete 1855 or the mystically effusive 1859, is its tone of aggressive bonhomie, almost of hilarity. Mr Kelley sees this as the result of the meliorist theories of contemporary socialism. I see it as the sort of joke that rapidly wears one out. For just as Baudelaire's elegance, as shown in Deroy's portrait of 1844, seems to carry a threat of built-in dilapidation, so his critical challenge to existing title-holders in 1846 seems decidedly quixotic. He is above all determined to arrive, whereas his true calling was to travel hopelessly. And in the 1840s, the disintegrating years of Romanticism no less than the years that marked the rise of Realism, the quickest way of arriving was to parody the advanced theories (both Romantic and Realist) of a man so far ahead of his public that he did not expect to see himself appreciated until the 1880s: Stendhal. Not only is the tone of the *Salon* of 1846 exaggeratedly *"frais et dispos"*, the shape, with its alternating short and long chapters, short and long sentences, is lifted without disguise from Stendhal's *Histoire de la peinture en Italie*. So unabashed is this parody, so deliberately does Baudelaire insert the most abrupt pronouncements, so simply does he adopt the whizzing speed of the older man, that the effect conveyed is one of radical chic.

To be fair, this impression comes from looking at the pages rather than actually reading them. But it is borne out by that inconsequential dedication, *"Aux Bourgeois"*. Was Baudelaire really a Utopian who believed that the world would be better when the men of property became men of taste? Or was he simply pointing them out as a section of society which did not even know a good thing when it was presented to it? The first, probably, for Baudelaire is never frivolous; the serious socialist, however, would prefer a more broadly based, less thinly aesthetic argument. And this is the extent of Baudelaire's venture into the political arena, if we exclude his confession, in this same *Salon*, that he occasionally had an overwhelming desire to flog the odd republican for his lack of respect for Watteau, or his hysterical behaviour in 1848, when he took advantage of the general effervescence to announce his intention of killing his stepfather. Perhaps we can read the dedication as a sort of familial threat, intricately bound up with the succeeding section on the function of criticism. Nothing much is announced here either, but the position of this short chapter at the beginning of the *Salon*, taking precedence over other aesthetic matters, and over all artists, would seem to indicate a gentle exercise in self-promotion at the expense of the uninitiated.

It is only in the section on Romanticism that Baudelaire seems prepared to lead us into the body of his argument, and even here our expectations are unfulfilled. For surely, in 1846, we can look for a definitive, even a retrospective, summation of what the Romantic endeavour was all about? Instead we are told what it is not about and teased with a Stendhalian insight on the relativity of beauty ("*Il y a autant de beautés qu'il y a de manières habituelles de chercher le bonheur*") which Baudelaire denatures slightly by advancing his own criteria for happiness, beauty, and Romanticism. These turn out to be intimacy, spirituality, aspiration towards the infinite, and colour. It is clear that the terms are becoming confused, that Baudelaire is not pursuing a sequential argument (he rarely does), and that his own satisfactions will be so inward-looking, pervasive, and at the same time insubstantial, that until he attaches them to something very concrete – i.e. the achievement of Delacroix – he will not be adding much to the Romantic debate. Indeed the only justification for continuing this debate lies in the fact that Delacroix, retreating rapidly from the overt Romantic statements he made before 1830, remained an awesome but increasingly distant presence until 1863.

The theory is that as Delacroix is still painting, Romanticism still lives. That Baudelaire has in a sense to trim and expand his definition of Romanticism to contain the personality of Delacroix matters not a bit. For in doing so he captures the melancholia of Romanticism in its terminal stages, when personal grief and anxiety have acquired a stoic disguise, when classical subject-matter is infused with the tension of the age, and when the quest for novelty has ceded to the stability of expecting nothing. All of this is implicit in the chapter on Delacroix, and explicit in the descriptions of pictures such as *Romeo's Farewell to Juliet* and *Les Femmes d'Alger*. Prophetic rather than critical, as

Baudelaire rightly describes his appraisal of Delacroix, his attachment to the distinction of the man and the beauty of the pictures will be sufficient, in future writings, to create a truly personal ideological system.

The effect of Delacroix on Baudelaire is to release him into a more straightforward exposition of his preferences. And the historical position is made clear only in Chapter 7, the section dealing with the ideal and the model. This apparently colourless title should be taken seriously, for it summons up the two shibboleths that had controlled the immovable classical programme.

The tyranny of the *beau idéal*, to which a painter as revolutionary as David had conformed, was the citadel against which the propagandists of the Romantic endeavour had flung their despairing weight. In France, so tenacious was the classical discipline of imitation of some Greco-Roman norm that of all the Romantic practitioners only Berlioz avoids a feeling of apostasy. Even Delacroix was embarrassed as being included among the Romantic iconoclasts. *"Je suis un pur classique"* was his tendentious riposte to a wrong-headed admirer, for his is a classicism imposed on and after the Romantic experiment. This guilt-ridden involvement with classicism (or more properly with the artistic movement known as Neoclassicism) persists throughout the entire French Romantic Movement, and it was left to Baudelaire, in 1846, to unearth the crucial objection for which all earlier propagandists had been seeking: *"Les poètes, les artistes, et toute la race humaine seraient bien malheureux, si l'idéal, cette absurdité, cette impossibilité était trouvé. Qu'est-ce que chacun ferait désormais de son pauvre moi?"* Submission to the rules, however golden, of the norm defeat the imperative desire to exist of the individual personality. Although every Romantic artist had been activated by the claims of the *"pauvre moi"*, none had stated so angrily as Baudelaire the need to have this fact generally accepted.

Having freed his own "moi" from its previously trammelled

existence, Baudelaire puts it to good use. Ingres, the apparent upholder of the classical rules and models, comes in for some brief but devastating disaffection. The judgements become brilliant and savage: Vernet, Scheffer, and many lesser men are practically guillotined out of existence. And when one turns to the illustrations of the pictures actually exhibited in the *Salon*, one wonders how anyone could have a good word – or indeed any kind of word – to say for them. Perhaps this artistic paucity goes some way to explaining the ruminative tendencies of most of the critics Mr Kelley quotes. Baudelaire of course needed no encouragement to speculate and project, and we are so used to his digressions that it is salutary to note how conscientiously he does his reporting work, although it usually takes him three-quarters of his space to get down to it. Priority must be given to his "*pauvre moi*". It is also the fact that his individual judgements are so correct, and have been ratified by posterity, that leads us to give credence to his intellectual stability. The apparent logic of his argument is deeply seductive. But when one has followed him to the end of the *Salon* of 1846 one does feel a premonitary qualm. How on earth is he to wind up his diatribe? How does one make a satisfactory concluding statement on a situation widely acknowledged to be provisional? If the forces of history are beating down on him as hard as Mr Kelley would suppose, can he avoid a historical pronouncement?

In Baudelaire's case, autobiographical preoccupation is the usual substitute and in fact serves him just as well. The final section of the *Salon* of 1846 is entitled "*De l'héroïsme de la vie moderne*", and it deals with the predicament of the artist born when the great traditions of the past are eroded and the pattern of the future is unclear. What will he use for subject-matter? Contemporary realism might be attractive; it might also turn out to be trivial. But as Baudelaire is both an artist himself and a Romantic of the terminal variety he is able to postulate a broken, precarious, but potentially glorious situation in which present change is infused with eternal insights. This is the moral and physical climate of *Les Fleurs du mal*, of *"Paris change! mais rien dans ma mélancholie n'a changé!"* And it is entirely appropriate that all Baudelaire's speculations in the last analysis apply only to himself.

That Baudelaire, in 1846, was engaged on the same task as a number of other art critics, Thoré and Champfleury among them, is a fact that should be borne in mind. But a quantitative analysis of their views obscures one vital difference, namely that Baudelaire went on to follow a different path.

In 1846 he is still able to surmount his own metaphysical system, one which, as it deepened, left no room for doubts and in which even calculations of probabilities were rigorously controlled. The word "temperament", thrown about fairly widely in 1846, soon comes to be grounded in sadness and what he calls aspiration towards the infinite. The only temperament he can fully appreciate is that possessed by Delacroix, and his critical method, as it evolves, is concerned with the promotion of this hero and the exclusion of others. The duality of nature and imagination, made explicit by the famous rivalry between Ingres and Delacroix, will take on a theological overtone: in the *Salon* of 1859 Baudelaire uses the telling phrase, *"l'évangile de la peinture"*. The differences between the *Salons* of 1846 and 1859 are those of precocious youth and premature old age. In Baudelaire's case this trajectory was short. But in his working-out of a rationale for his own conception of beauty the *Salon* of 1846 proved to be a valuable arena. And the high spirits should not be ignored. They show him, for once in his beleaguered life, making the best of things.

8

The Master of the Attributions*

BEYOND THE PALE OF Settlement, that 1,000-mile strip of territory that once stretched through Imperial Russia and its provinces from the Baltic to the Black Sea, lies the world, as much symbolic as geographical, where the possibilities of advancement are infinite, even if they denature the traveller who desires to exchange one custom for another. For such a traveller there can be no return. The small amount of residual nostalgia he may feel he will willingly renounce for what other people, other citizens, possess as of right: freedom to travel and to prosper, freedom to impose. What he will lose for ever is the sense of belonging in a context in which his true reality and significance are understood. Speaking many languages, he will forgo his native tongue. Such a traveller was Bernhard (later Bernard) Berenson, doyen of the world's most mandarin profession, *grand seigneur*, doge of the unattributed fifteenth-century *predella* panel, passionate sightseer and permanent exile.

He was born in 1865 in the province of Vilna in Lithuania, in a village so obscure that there seems to be no agreed spelling of its name. At the age of ten he emigrated with his family to America. A photograph taken during his year at Boston University shows a naïf but determined face, with gleaming eyes, a full mouth, and luxuriant

*Meryle Secrest: *Being Bernard Berenson. A Biography*. Weidenfeld & Nicolson; Ernest Samuels: *Bernard Berenson. The Making of A Connoisseur*. Harvard University Press. *The Times Literary Supplement*, 18 January 1980.

Pre-Raphaelite hair. The date is 1884. Nearly twenty years later, behold the finished man in his Italian villa: correctly tailored, shorn, elegant, the extravagances pared away. He was to become ever more dapper and meticulous, smaller, one would say, until at the end, at the age of ninety-four, he could be carried about in his nurse's arms.

The Jews of Vilna were famous for their learning, but that learning was not secular. Knowledge of the Haskalah or Enlightenment movement was limited to a few, and these were thought to be not holy. Of the 613 commandments which a pious Jew must fulfil Berenson was to remember only the tabulation. He made lists, or rather the Lists – of Venetian, Florentine, Umbrian and Milanese pictures – which have served generations of students as the essential map of Renaissance painting. Like Winckelmann, whom he so much resembled, he left the inimical north for the warm sun of Italy, changing his religion en route, and for the sins he committed under the aegis of Haskalah he was rewarded with the admiration of the world and the veneration of aesthetes and collectors. Like Winckelmann he lived in great style; unlike Winckelmann he died in his bed, for his enemies – and he had many – were not there at the end. Nobody knows whether he found the heresy by which he lived any easier to sustain than the orthodoxy he abandoned. Neither Berenson himself nor his two excellent biographers have anything to reveal on this point.

Like Winckelmann, Berenson created his own theology, a theology that survived without the help of metaphysics. Like Winckelmann's, his method was an affair of personal vocation based on ethically shaky foundations. His disregard for documents, his taste for the numinous, and his neo-Morellian divinations defined him as a phenomenon, rather like a prestidigitator or a clairvoyant. It is surprising that so much of his activity turned into art history and opened the eyes of so many disciples (the word is used advisedly). What is not surprising is that it has worn so badly and has not survived the perfecting of techniques such as the X-raying of successive layers of paint on a panel or a canvas, or the refinement of analysis of pigment. The oracular pronouncements with which Berenson could once either promote or relegate a work of art no longer hold good; we have entered the era of semantics.

His status as *stupor mundi* was early revealed at Harvard, where he followed courses in Greek, Latin, Arabic, Sanskrit, philosophy (under William James), and the art of the Middle Ages and the Renaissance under Charles Eliot Norton, one of whose friends, Isabella Stewart Gardner, was to prove a decisive influence in Berenson's life.

His aspirations at this stage were towards literature, and he contributed an extraordinary range of articles to the *Harvard Monthly*, and also wrote a few short stories which are the only intimate documents of his whole opaque life. He desired all sorts of excellence, the first step towards which would take him to Oxford and to Europe. Surprisingly he failed to obtain a travelling scholarship, but private funds were contributed by his friends, teachers and Mrs Gardner to make up a purse of 700 dollars. In 1887 Berenson left America for his Grand Tour. He did indeed go to Oxford, where he failed to make the personal acquaintance of Walter Pater, whose writings he admired. Since it was already Berenson's intention to burn with a hard gem-like flame, this was perhaps regrettable. But there were compensations. In 1888 he met Mary Costelloe, who was to become his wife twelve years later. And then there was the whole continent of Europe: Paris with its theatres, Munich and Bayreuth with their opera, and finally Italy with its pictures.

In the spring of 1889, after months of enchanted wandering, Berenson reached Florence. His desire now was "to encompass the art of Italy", and this he more or less did. The money ran out, but friends could be persuaded to subsidize him. Only Mrs Gardner appears to have been nettled by the delayed return of her protégé. Their correspondence, too rapturous for her taste, was broken off. In the meantime Berenson, a tireless traveller, visited the towns and cities, the villages and hamlets, the churches and obscure convents of the mainland. His prodigious memory filed away details of a painting's appearance, its possible connection with one seen elsewhere, its association with a great network of undiscovered masterpieces languishing far from the appreciative eye. In abandoned chapels, Berenson, on a ladder, holding up a candle, would find, examine, and commit to memory. He seems to have been indifferent to the import of a single work. It was the pilgrimage that obsessed him. In his *Sketch for a Self-Portrait*, written in 1941, he reports a crucial conversation with Enrico Costa in Bergamo, in which he decided to devote his life to connoisseurship, with "no idea, no ambition, no expectation, no thought of reward . . . We must not stop until we are sure that every Lotto is a Lotto, every Cariani a Cariani, every Santacroce a Santacroce etc."

And this he did. If his attributions have not always stood the test of time, if those made-up artists Amico di Sandro and Alunno di Domenico have been quietly disbanded, there is no doubt that we now know many more hundreds, maybe thousands, of Italian pictures than we would have done if Berenson had not made his home and his life in Italy. His "method", which to us today may seem almost distastefully magical, was based on the precepts of Morelli, whom he met in Milan in 1901, and the pragmatism of William James, whose lectures he had attended at Harvard. Morelli, trained as a doctor in Berlin, perfected the morphological investigation of phenomena, and learned to recognize a painter's signature in the curl of an ear, the angle of a finger, and the fall of a wave of hair. In Berenson's hands comparative anatomy became connoisseurship; in a very short period of time his faultless memory could connect these noses and fingers and waves of hair across a continent. Artistic personalities grew where none had previously existed; a painter's life could be traced from early to late work. Nor was this accomplished mechanically. Pictures had a curious effect on Berenson, which he was only able to explain in clumsy but well-worn terms.

He found them, and by extension other aspects of existence, "life-enhancing". This is not a mere *fin-de-siècle* flourish. In his occasionally severe phraseology he explains, in *Florentine Painters of the Renaissance*, that "art stimulates to an unwonted activity psychical processes which are in themselves the source of most (if not all) of our pleasures, and which here, free from disturbing sensations, never tend to pass over into pain".

This mysterious process will be triggered by a realization of a picture's "tactile values", again explored in *Florentine Painters*, and again a humdrum description of an important psychological, or, as he would say, "psychical" activity. Just as an infant learns to make of touch the test of reality, so is it the painter's business to continue this attempt to make sense of the world by giving tactile values to retinal sensations. For painting is about duplicity; it has only two dimensions. It is the triumph of the painter to create three, and his power is thereby disproportionately great. A painter's first business is "to rouse the tactile sense, for I must have the illusion of varying muscular sensations inside my palm and fingers, corresponding to the various projections of this figure, before I shall take it for granted as real, *and let it affect me lastingly* [my italics]".

This experience, and others analogous to it, will produce "ideated sensations", another clumsy term, which may be nothing more than an updated and falsely rational equivalent of Stendhal's *"illusion parfaite"*, the process whereby a work of art could activate the experience of perfect happiness glimpsed in other times and places, usually without immediate or apparent causation. For Stendhal, happiness was love, or being in love, a brave practice which he carried on fruitlessly all his life. For the equally romantic but much more circumspect Berenson, happiness was a feeling of mystical union with creation, which he called, even more disastrously than usual, "IT-ness". This explains not only his protean gifts, of which he quickly tired, but the eventual transmutation of his love of art into a love of nature, perhaps his most impressive characteristic. *"Dahin! Dahin!"* he exclaimed with Goethe, and in his Italian dream journeyed, almost religiously, on and on, to the next town, the next village, and the next picture.

Unfortunately it all took money, and Berenson, still living on his friends, clearly could not be called to account. But in 1892 he managed to secure for his friend James Burke a picture by Piero di Cosimo for 200 pounds less than the agreed price. Burke made over to him that 200 pounds. In the spring of 1893 he discouraged a party of Americans in Rome from squandering money on doubtful pictures and received a commission. Any qualms he might have felt at these transactions were quickly dispelled by his now constant companion Mary Costelloe, who had left her husband and daughters to devote her life to Berenson. A large cheery feminist, Mary was already known in England for her secretaryship of the Women's Christian Temperance Union, her advocacy of women's suffrage and the election of women to county councils, and her lecture on "The Position of Women in America". Forthright, exuberant and determined, Mary was undoubtedly life-enhancing. She urged Berenson to publish and typed away at his notes; when his *Venetian Painters of the Renaissance* appeared in 1894 she wrote laudatory articles under the name of Mary Logan. The money began to come in.

But it did not really come in until a copy of *Venetian Painters* was sent to Mrs Gardner, who had recently inherited two million dollars and was determined to collect Old Masters, "only the greatest in the world". In 1895 Berenson agreed to advise Mrs Gardner for a fee of five per cent. That same year he acquired for her twenty major paintings through Colnaghi's alone, Otto Gutekunst acting as the commercial agent. In 1897 he bought for her a Van Dyck, a Cima (later called "after"), a Titian (now Sanchez Coello), a Correggio ("influenced by"), a Crivelli, and two *cassone* panels by Pesellino. In 1898 he further acquired for her a Giorgione, a Rubens, the Inghirami Raphael, three Rembrandts, a Cellini bust, a Terborch, and a Masaccio; in 1899 two

Holbeins, a Fra Angelico, a Rembrandt, a Fiorenzo da Lorenzo, a Raphael, and the Chigi Botticelli. By this date he was also advising Theodore Davis and Ned Warren, former friends from his Boston days. He continued to publish. Mary was "simply overwhelmed with Bernhard's genius". Mrs Gardner demanded an "adorable" Velázquez and a "heavenly" Raphael, and he knew where to find them.

He married Mary in 1900, by which time they were both Catholics and both lapsed. Depression and ill-health began to settle in from this date and were to plague him for the rest of his life. Mary's cheeriness was undiminished. Owing to Berenson's horror of children she had an abortion at the end of 1901, and wrote to him from London, "I wish thee felt half as jolly as I am feeling now that the Anxiety is removed." She was a slapdash and extravagant housekeeper, and more money was needed. By now Berenson was financing his whole family in Boston, and he wanted a house of his own, that "great good place" that was to become the Villa I Tatti and which he was later to bequeath to Harvard. A triumphal tour of America in 1903 indicated how the money could be earned. A word from Berenson could add to or diminish the value of a painting; a recommendation from Berenson could secure a masterpiece from a hallowed private collection for an American museum. He became famous and rich.

But still more money was needed, and at this point the sense of IT-ness seems to have become impaired by the necessities of commerce. Some time in 1906 Berenson changed sides and from being the buyer's advocate became the seller's. He joined forces with Duveen for a fee of twenty-five per cent. As all Duveen's sales were gilt-edged, heavily restored and occasionally phoney, Berenson became enmeshed in those dubious business practices that flourished while the rage to collect swept across America and which still hedge his name with an aura of compromise. It is still not clear how much commission he took from whom, but it was a great deal. "Trading up" became habitual. One goal, that of excellence, was exchanged for another: the acquisition and embellishment of I Tatti, and the extension of himself as a work of art.

The activities, the journeyings, and the business dealings of Berenson and Mary became demonic. Their equilibrium suffered. Mary developed a number of distressing ailments; she put on weight and became slightly hysterical. Berenson, on the other hand, became smaller, tighter, and more cautious. There is some evidence that he found his position untenable, although he was not to be freed from it until extreme old age. His autobiographical *Sketch for a Self-Portrait* fails to come to terms with the truth and races off on tangents and into anecdotes at the slightest opportunity. Either he does not know himself or he puts up a resistance to knowing himself that would defy professional analysis. Mrs Secrest chronicles but cannot throw much light on this aspect of his life. She also chronicles the ups and downs of the Berenson marriage. Mary was attracted to younger men. Berenson was apparently irresistible to women, although his own affections seem to have been slight, mean, and routine.

Ladies came and went, among them the stunning Gladys Deacon, and his injured self-esteem was slightly mended by their flattering insistence on hearing him discourse. When Mary died in 1945 she had long been replaced by the adoring Nicky Mariano, his devoted companion and housekeeper, who slept outside the door of his room when he felt ill. In her care Berenson ended his days, and his last years were becalmed by her presence and the recovery of a sense of IT-ness which, as it is expressed in the late diaries, is nothing short of miraculous.

For the rest he is an unsatisfactory but important figure. For he did something different with and for art. He did not look to it for consolation or for redemption or as a vehicle for a higher morality. Unlike his model, Pater, he did not use it to express his own unsatisfied desires. Pater on Botticelli has slender but painful insights, recognizing in *The Birth of Venus* a melancholy that mirrors his own: ". . . what is

unmistakable is the sadness with which he [Botticelli] has conceived
the goddess of pleasure, as a depository of a great power over the lives
of men."

In comparison Berenson is brisk and intuitive. He does not yearn,
but clings tenaciously to the formal rhythm of this work. "The movement is directly life-communicating. The entire picture presents us
with the quintessence of all that is pleasurable to the imagination of
touch and movement." He has re-established the picture as an object
to be scrutinized for what the artist put there, and not for what the
critic found there. Art history has learnt new techniques and many
more words since his day. But as a model, journeying, crossing and
re-crossing Italy, examining, questioning, remembering, he has not
been surpassed.

Nor should he be. A sense of IT-ness is not within the reach of
all, but it is good to be reminded of it. Berenson, at the approach
of death, learned to use his eye more lovingly. Self, not easily laid
aside in his case, gave way from time to time to a blessed receptivity.
Despite the considerable efforts and fine scholarship of his two biographers it is only fair to let Berenson have the last word, written in his
ninetieth year:

> On balcony this morning between 4.15 and 4.45, flat
> quiet light, mother-of-pearl tone with touches here
> and there of rose in the sky. Water oily, seemed to be
> flowing in but drift went the other way. The Salute
> like an engraving, or rather an etching, Whistlerish.
> Watched the gradual lighting-up until I was too tired
> to wait for the full sunlight illuminating the entire
> sky. Giovanni Bellini and his immediate followers
> painted landscapes as if they did them at dawn,
> probably because they realized the impossibility of
> doing sunshine. They paint the pallid sunless sky in

the evocative way that delights us in even such mediocrities as Basaiti or Bissolo. In Bellini himself the skies are always of pale dawn, except in the Berlin *Resurrection*, where he gives us a sky with crimson cloudlets that revive and inspire us with a fellow-feeling for Him who rose from the dead as triumphant as the sun over darkness.

9

The Eye of Innocence*

IN PHOTOGRAPHS COROT APPEARS as a bluff ugly man with a
determined jaw, tired eyes, and a disillusioned mouth. In the self-
portrait he painted in 1835 he looks unfinished, clumsy, in marked
contrast to his elaborate velvet cap and his spotless painting overall.
The point of the self-portrait is this overall, which is described in thick
matte stretches of subtle mushroom-coloured paint. Both tone and
texture bring to mind Chardin, whose name is invariably pressed into
service whenever Corot is under discussion. The mouth and the eyes
give nothing away. Like Chardin, too, is Corot the public man, given to
seraphic utterances, acts of charity, counsels of mercy, and an assumption of innocence of the ways of this world. Yet even Chardin, as he
painted himself at the end of his life, has a faintly irascible appearance.

The problem with both painters is to discern the powerful professional conscience behind the self they presented to the world, a critical
act which may seem indelicate to some, for the projected self is so
unusually good, so angelic, that the weariest kind of scepticism seems
called for in order to dismantle it. Yet it must be admitted that both
Chardin and Corot are at least as clever as the pictures they painted.
No child of nature, no St Vincent de Paul of painting, as Corot
was called, could have encompassed so many striking innovations,
could have established a tradition within a tradition, unless endowed
with some measure of originality, fearlessness, subtlety, and supreme

* Jean Leymarie: *Corot*. Skira / Macmillan. *The Times Literary Supplement*, 21 March 1980.

calculation. To investigate these qualities is not necessarily a loveless task. Yet it is one which many art historians avoid.

Corot in particular presents a challenge, for at first sight he would appear to be the only unproblematic painter of the nineteenth century, as remote from political struggle or the crisis of faith or the dangers and attractions of Romanticism as it is possible to be. For these very reasons – and for the apparent absence of conflict in his works – he has been rewarded by posterity with gratitude, and for these reasons too the critical literature on him is extremely sparse.

The facts of his life are thin and consist mainly of the dates of his various journeys. He never married, was good to his friends, and died at an appropriate age. Amateurs, content with these facts, and, it must be said, tranquillized out of a hunt for clues by the very equilibrium which his pictures bestow, have in the main sought no further. The art historian Jean Leymarie's monograph, first published in 1966, is in this indulgent and readable tradition. Yet nobody to date has got the measure of Corot. As well as being the most accessible of nineteenth-century painters he is the most mysterious.

If we are to allow that he is not as simple as he looks, we must also allow that he regarded painting as the learned profession it undoubtedly is. Again we must allow that his masters were of little use to him, and that he composed his style from a powerful natural vision, yet that this vision was not arrived at by means of serendipity. Indeed the first critical problem arises with his masters, for in their efforts to make these masters relevant historians are soon led into references to the classical tradition which, strictly speaking, have nothing to do with the case. They are then faced with the multiplicity of Corot's styles, which burgeon from an early synthesis of amazing singularity and power and eventually meet up with all the main trends in French art of the second half of the nineteenth century.

It is of course the early Corot that most people know, and it is the early Corot who presents the greatest difficulty. Those calmly lucent yet infernally hot scenes of Avignon and Rome, allegedly composed according to an established but in fact untraceable formula, were painted before Corot was thirty. He had fifty more years of work in front of him, yet at no time does he venture more hardily or succeed more decisively. Thus Corot scholarship faces its biggest problem at the very outset of the painter's career: the easier part comes last of all.

This problem has been dealt with in the usual way. Tradition dictates that in order to explain Corot's style it is necessary to rush forward a number of names of landscape painters who have nothing in common either with each other or with Corot, apart from the fact that they painted landscapes. There is a certain desperation in this activity, for the most cursory glance will reveal that Corot owes very little to Joseph Vernet (who painted detailed scenes of Rome and the ports of France), to David (who painted only one landscape in the whole of his career), to those shadowy characters Michallon and Bertin, who were his official masters, to Valenciennes, the strange painter who seemed for a time to prefigure his starkly simplified vision, or to his contemporaries, Granet and Ingres.

The situation is further complicated by the fact that from early middle age onwards Corot did in fact take into account the works of certain contemporary painters such as Rousseau and Troyon, particularly the latter, while the work of his protracted and extraordinary old age is a set of variations on motifs furnished by almost anyone, from Raphael to Monet.

What is baffling about him is his reticence, both verbal and painterly, about what started him off and brought him to such rapid maturity. As M. Leymarie points out, the *View of Lausanne* of 1825 is already a mature Corot and it was painted on the way to Italy. Yet according to one line of argument it was only in Italy that Corot matured, ingesting the classical tradition in order to bring it back, three years later, to France, and thus provide the missing link between Claude and Cézanne (names which are cited by M. Leymarie). Of all the artists invoked these last two are the least relevant, as are the terms classical and romantic. If Corot is a problem it is not to those who look at him but to those who write about him, because he clearly does not belong where he has been put, and also perhaps because he was wily and secretive and so assured that he never felt the need to explain himself or to gull a credulous contemporary into popularizing his "struggle".

Corot's struggle was not with the classical tradition or the legacy of his immediate predecessors but with the bewildering multiplicity of things seen. A typical, that is to say an early, Corot will always present the spectator with less than the eye actually encompasses, unlike a Constable, which will harry the mind with more than is normally perceived. For Corot the mind is at the service of the eye, to modulate, to control, to unify and to present. The result will be a moderately sized canvas showing an ideally distanced but not remote view of a town or site. This will be extremely calm, and populated by only one or two figures. The viewpoint will be high, as if the artist were looking out of a window across an intervening space. A strange dreamy, creamy placidity will be achieved, as if the site were viewed under an immobile and cloudless sky on an uneventful afternoon. This impression – but the word gives a misleadingly hasty resonance to what was in fact a fixed idea – will be achieved by mixing all the colours with white. Architecture, whether the Hospice at Villeneuve, or the Cabassud houses at Ville d'Avray, will be unaccented, flatly frontal, blind, eschewing surface accidents and details. The result will be an image of extraordinary clarity and peace, strong enough to becalm the spectator into thinking that he too might find so tranquil a scene. He will not, for it does not exist in nature.

This kind of synthesis, created in about 1825 and sustained for some twenty years, had in fact been achieved by earlier painters, but they were not French, had nothing to do with the classical tradition or indeed with any other, used a different medium, and left a relatively small body of work. One of these may have been Girtin, the English watercolourist, whose view of the Porte Saint-Denis in Paris possesses many of the features that characterize a mature Corot. Another was certainly Bonington, the timely expatriate who introduced so many English novelties to French painters through the medium of his work for Baron Taylor's *Voyages pittoresques dans l'ancienne France*, and who was probably better understood in France than the restless and complex Constable. In his confessional old age, when he divulged some of his many borrowings, Corot painted the superb *Belfry at Douai*, which is a reprise of Bonington's *Market Tower at Bergues* in the Wallace Collection; and more comparisons could be found between the hardened professional of seventy-nine and the innovator of twenty-four.

Girtin and Bonington are mysterious painters. Both did their most original work in France, both died very young, yet both possessed a totally assured idiom. It was through their suggestions, it would seem, that Corot achieved the miraculous focusing of his chosen site. In certain instances, notably in the scenes of Paris and its bridges, Corot's vision was copied by the young Monet and the young Renoir, thus ensuring a school of landscape painting free from the pervasive and somewhat inharmonious influences of Constable and Ruysdael, or even that, so piously recorded, of Claude. In his turn, and many years later, Corot was to look with fascination and with melancholy at the huge figure paintings of the young Impressionists, and to reproduce them, veiled in a pervasive gloom, as figures in his studio. In this way an internal core of tradition, rooted entirely in nineteenth-century discoveries, emerges from a school of painting in which anxiety about the present and desire for the stability of the past are often all too obvious.

The enigmatic equilibrium of the early works was not prolonged. The assured or typical Corot dissolves somewhere around 1855 and is replaced by a painter of fashionably misty nymphs, dancing or playing tambourines in very dim forest clearings, beneath trees bending at an angle of forty-five degrees and furnished with the statutory weight of foliage. These works, designed to harmonize with the tastes of the Second Empire, are still persuasive. A bourgeois daintiness on a fairly massive scale distinguishes these canvases from everything that went before or was to come after. The light of noon is replaced by the grey of twilight; solidity has given way to wispiness. These pictures of the 1850s were tremendously popular and were admired by the Emperor and his court; they may be seen as a pious and crafty interlude in the life and work of Corot. They won him a medal. It was at about this time that he began to voice characteristic thoughts: i.e. Delacroix "is an eagle and I am but a lark singing my little song in my grey clouds".

Yet even in this period, in which he spent as much time at the ballet as he did in the countryside, he was able to paint the *Church at Marissel* (1866) and the magnificent *Bridge at Mantes* (1867), in which the lead steeple of the one and the matt stone arches of the other are softened by the now curving or leaning trunks of stripped poplars: souvenirs, as he would have said, of his recent sentimentality, an experiment markedly at odds with the unassuming rigour of his early works.

Thus the Corot of the middle period, the 1850s and 1860s, can be seen to relax comfortably into the prevailing atmosphere of Rococo nostalgia. Yet he was too much of a painter and not enough of a man of the world to be satisfied with his new and limited perspective. And besides, having entered the arena of official art exhibitions, he could not remain in ignorance of the efforts, sometimes subversive, of younger painters. He was to emerge from this middle phase, in which he combined the naturalistic with the artificial, and to change his style yet again, this time concentrating on his contemporaries, on established masters, and on the recently dead. He gave an impression of healthiness and sturdiness which must have been partly assumed, for a note of melancholy, always discernible in his fiercely lonely figures – monks, nuns, children, brides – becomes deeper, merging with studies popularized by other painters.

A man in armour, his eyes cast down, recalls Meissonier. A woman and a child in a clearing in a wood remind one of Renoir. A bathing nymph, after Courbet, tends her hair. Mlle Goldschmidt, called *The Lady with the Pearl*, is painted in the style of the Mona Lisa. Mlle Foudras, a muslin blouse over her black working dress, her deeply shadowed eye-sockets staring sombrely at the spectator, is one of Delacroix's *Femmes d'Alger*. A woman half-undressed, her book in her lap, is as self-contained, as remote as an early Degas. The *Lady in Blue* of 1874, chin in pensive hand, is a version of Monet's *Camille*, exhibited in the *Salon* of 1866. In all these works the light is muted, wintry. In the painter's studio, models, perhaps inspired by Vermeer (a recent rediscovery), sit listlessly before an easel. Yet outside in nature, which at last looks like nature, the grey calm afternoon draws on, and the road to Sin le Noble gives back the reassuring image of a style as close to home and as independent of the paintings of other artists as were those of Chardin in the eighteenth century.

There have been a number of books on Corot but no major study. Corot defeats written analysis much as Chardin did, and for the same reasons. His last words, frequently quoted, are reported to have been, "*Je voudrais que vous voyiez ces immenses horizons.*" Perhaps he saw the human condition as sad and lonely and childlike, as his figure paintings would suggest, and managed to divorce this from his concept of nature, which always gave him release. "*Il n'a pas assez souvent le diable au corps,*" complained Baudelaire, who thought that the prospect of nature should always throw one into a paroxysm of disgust. Corot's mastery, whether it sprang from innocence or control, was also an unvoiced criticism of Romantic introspection. It was the nearest involvement he ever permitted himself in contemporary affairs, and, as with everything else, he kept it well hidden.

10

The Last of the Old Masters *

"*LE JOUR DE LA revanche viendra pour Courbet aussi . . . On lui ouvrira les portes du Louvre, et l'heure de son apothéose sonnera.*" So wrote Zola in 1878 in a very beautiful passage aimed at the artistic establishment which had omitted to arrange a Courbet retrospective at the Exposition Universelle of that year. The hour of the apotheosis has now struck, and the magnificence of Courbet is now revealed. The irony is that at the Grand Palais and now at the Royal Academy he appears as the last of the Old Masters, whereas in 1855 he set himself up at the gates of the Exposition Universelle of that year as the first of the dissidents.

Zola saw Delacroix, Ingres and Courbet as the three greatest painters of the nineteenth century, and percipiently held to this view throughout the changes and chances wrought by the Impressionists and the Symbolists. He saw a grandeur in Courbet's personality that qualified him for immortality, and adored the truculence of his quasi-heroic behaviour. Courbet's innocent cunning – his refusal to admit to any specific masters or influences – and fearless nihilistic independence presented an embodiment of Zola's far more nervous dreams writ large.

Despite the noisy affirmations in paint and print, we do not, however, quite know how Courbet saw himself. How much was that truculence inspired by the provincial's envy of the reclusive but

* *The Times Literary Supplement*, 27 January 1978.

dangerous Delacroix, the iron-willed Ingres, the graceful and insanely popular Delaroche? How much was it inspired by the urgent demands of the dispossessed classes after 1848? How much by emulation of Daumier and Millet, those much more subversive agents of anger and pity? In comparison with these artists Courbet seems jocose and opaque, magnificently protected against injustice by the health of his body and his simple and impermeable mind. Perhaps his constant and only "message" is the centrality of Courbet, with hazy tangential references to the solidarity of the workers and the dignity of art. Perhaps Realism, the programme to which he is historically attached, is for him not a platform but the only phenomenon he could accept. *"Courbet, maître-peintre, sans idéal et sans religion"*, stated his letter-head. These are fighting words, but in fact may not amount to much more than making a virtue of necessity. For one who has no sense of ambiguity, no awareness, not necessarily of the transcendental but of the random, Realism is not a doctrine but the very air he breathes.

Hence that world of pungent women, of euphoric half-drunk men. It is the world of the four-hour lunch, of the evening spent tippling, of harsh sexual teasing, and not much else. Mme Grégoire, the light glinting on her well-fed face, is patroness of this festival. Rumpled sleazy girls, exhibiting their cheap mittens and their white stockings to the shocked spectator, overweight *baigneuses*, Regis Courbet snoozing after dinner in his malodorous but convivial kitchen, trout the size of carp, yards of female hair, sniggering all-male parties, damp-fleshed nudes, an amazing tendency for everyone to fall asleep: all this signals a consciousness at ease as long as the flesh is buoyant, a near absence of thought. This contention is borne out by the fact that with the encroachment of illness Courbet declined immediately as a painter and as a personality. Imprisoned in Sainte Pélagie, he seems to be waiting politely for help. And exiled to La Tour de Peilz, that silent pretty village where it seems to be always dusk, he contributes less to the history of art than to the mythology of boozing.

Yet it must be remembered that we know very little about him, and probably always shall, for his sister Juliette destroyed all his papers after his death. Perhaps, for all his outrageous vanity, he was a defensive man. With perseverance one can find in him a thread of gravity. That portrait of Berlioz, as watchful, as distanced as might have been his doctor father at the bedside of a dying man; Mme de Brayer, emerging from shadow with an immanence worthy of Chassériau; the hooked trout with agonized human eyes; a sad and lonely picture of apples with a pewter tankard; a coldly red sunset over Lake Geneva; a modulation from complacency to reticence in the portraits: all, admittedly, are dragged down by the copious use of bitumen, but they nevertheless constitute a departure from the compulsively sociable figurehead that Courbet decided to be for the benefit of his friends. And very little of this has anything to do with philosophies of art.

To make sense out of Realism, the movement which has so bedevilled and in some cases falsified assessment of Courbet, is the task of the historian. But one thing is certain: Realism emerges from Romanticism as the child emancipates itself from the parent. Courbet himself began his painting career well within the Romantic tradition of the *grande machine*, adhering to the same scale and colour values as those used by David and Gros. His early self-portraits, with their amorous self-regard, their insistent confrontation of the author's personality with that of the spectator, are not too far distant in format from Géricault's late portrait of *Le Vendéen*, or Delacroix's self-portrait of *c.* 1837 in the Louvre. Realism may well have seemed the contemporary alternative to Romanticism, which dated rapidly because of its recognizable and in many cases obsolescent subject-matter. Hence the insistence in the 1840s on the demands of the "modern", demands met to a certain extent by Realism.

But this was no easy alternative. Champfleury, the critic who was

Courbet's most insistent champion, wrote in the preface to his novel, *Monsieur de Boisdhyver*, *"le métier de chercheur de la Réalité est peut-être plus dur que celui de bûcheron."* The image of the woodcutter is significant and perhaps ostentatiously popular; it is certainly quite irrelevant to the gentle tempo of Champfleury's story. Less gentle is Flaubert's treatment of Madame Bovary, that born Romantic martyred in the cause of Realism. It is only Flaubert's fastidious irony that elevates her into anything like distinction. Socially she is of the same milieu as Courbet's *Demoiselles de village*. In none of these cases is there any of that regard for popular causes that is said to distinguish Realism from its élitist predecessors. And despite the plain speaking of Courbet's intentions, his is in no sense demotic painting. His subject-matter may be drawn from the pastimes and preoccupations of the labouring classes – hence the anxiety it aroused in a predominantly bourgeois public – but these are in all cases subjected to a purely pictorial conscience.

If that pictorial conscience seems uneven, if some of the images remain blank, that too is well within the Realist programme. The brothers Goncourt made a telling mistake in *Manette Salomon*, their novel about the Paris art world in the 1840s and 1850s. Coriolis, the painter-hero, sends two would-be Realist works to the *Salon* of 1855. Lovingly described by the brothers, these fictitious canvases bristle with plot and sub-plot. They are anecdotal, and Realist composition is episodic. Many of Courbet's images have an accidental quality. In *Le Treillis*, for example, carnations, convolvulus, tiger lilies and phlox crowd into the front plane of the picture, eating up the air, while a hefty but curiously insubstantial girl tends them somewhere off to the right. Champfleury in his portraits looks downwards to the least important angle of the picture. Gamekeepers near Ornans stride across our field of vision and keep their purpose to themselves. This maddened Delacroix. *"Que veulent ces deux figures?"* was his unanswered (and unanswerable) question when he saw the notorious

Baigneuses. To this day art historians are striving to interpret the large and frightening picture called, variously, *La Toilette* (or *Le Repos*) *de la mariée* (or *de la morte*).

If there is a disappointing side to Courbet it lies in the loss of affect that his limited objectives entail. A case could be made out for his being as faithful to the inside of his head as Delacroix was to the inside of his, but Courbet did not remain puzzled by what was beyond his experience; he actively denied that anything outside his experience had any validity or indeed existence. The loss of affect is shared not by his historical champion Champfleury but by his moral champion Zola. One suspects that both saw Realism as a function of virility and adapted their styles accordingly.

To materialists Courbet must be the quintessential painter. Beyond the damaged enigma of the paint there is nothing that is not available. There is nothing redemptive either. But to use this term immediately takes one into the painful territory inhabited by Baudelaire, with whom, incredibly enough, Courbet at one point shared lodgings. In the portrait in Montpellier Courbet saw his friend as an uneasy mixture of monk and galley-slave. In the *Salon* of 1855 Baudelaire dismissed Courbet with a politeness worthy of Delacroix. *"Sans idéal et sans religion"* is an existential programme, valid only for the length of time one is capable of sustaining the fully responsible and responsive attitude to life that such a proposition entails. At the Royal Academy can be seen both its great virtues and its nagging defects.

II

Incantation to Inertia *

IT MAY BE A mistake to build generalizations on the example of one
man's work, particularly if that man is as isolated and as curious as
Gustave Moreau, and, one might add, so little known. This tendency,
which developed within a few years of his death, impelled partisans of
various causes to claim him, variously, as the last of the Romantics,
the first of the Surrealists, the archetypal Symbolist, or the precursor
of Fauvism. His highly personal idiom has both gained and lost
from this endeavour, which shows no sign of abating. Further glosses
have been added to his work by a totally different coterie, men of
letters who could not resist the compulsion to embellish his own
descriptions of his works. Despite Moreau's protestations that he was
not a literary painter, it seems that none of his contemporaries could
contemplate his pictures without bursting into fevered descriptions of
the mystery before their eyes, thus adding a further layer of impene-
trability to the limp but encrusted images which are, they agree,
profoundly allegorical.

Readers of Huysmans' *À rebours* may in fact only know Moreau
as the painter who best satisfied the immobile but delirious Des
Esseintes, intent on imbibing sensation without moving a muscle
to procure it. Contemplation of *Salome Dancing before Herod* would
reward Des Esseintes with a satisfying reminder of *"l'immortelle*

*Pierre-Louis Mathieu, *Gustave Moreau*. Complete Edition of the Finished Paintings,
Watercolours and Drawings. Phaidon. *The Times Literary Supplement*, 18 March 1977.

Hystérie", although he performed his connoisseur's task by setting down a list of Moreau's sources. In 1886, two years after the publication of *À rebours*, Ary Renan published a couple of articles in the respectable *Gazette des beaux-arts* which are touched with the same immortal hysteria, for Moreau seems to have induced a mild inflammation of the brain in those who try to claim him as their own. The present monograph by Pierre-Louis Mathieu is not free of these colonizing tendencies but it performs a valuable service; if it does nothing to demystify Moreau it does at least make him seem duller and more restricted to a single idiom than his earlier apologists would allow.

His life, to which M. Mathieu devotes too little space, is apparently devoid of mystery. After the death of a sister, Moreau remained the only child of devoted and well-to-do parents, who gave him every encouragement; his mother, in fact, accompanied him on his two-year study tour of Italy, while his father stayed at home in the rue de la Rochefoucauld (latterly the Musée Gustave Moreau), passing judgement on the well-filled sketchbooks which came back regularly through the post.

After exceedingly brief apprenticeships with the academic Picot and the romantic Chassériau, Moreau allowed his style to accumulate from a variety of sources. He exhibited at most of the Salons from 1852 to 1880, and attracted particular attention at the Salon of 1865 with his picture entitled *Le jeune homme et la mort*, which he dedicated to the memory of Chassériau and which sets the tone for his later elaborations on this theme: an elegy in which a martyred youth, reminiscent in attitude of St Sebastian, is ushered out of this world by a female presence with distinctly vampirish implications.

Moreau never married, choosing to remain with his mother, and when she became deaf he would communicate with her by handing her notebooks inscribed with statements like *"Il faut penser la couleur."* His mistress was billeted round the corner in the rue Notre Dame de Lorette. After the deaths of these two women he went into a decline from which he was rescued by an invitation to teach at the École des Beaux-Arts; his pupils included Rouault, the first curator of the museum he left to the nation. Other pupils were Camoin, Marquet, Manguin and Matisse.

To all intents and purposes it was an unlived life, which recommended itself highly to other masters of the unlived life such as Huysmans, Laforgue and Proust. Yet it contains its own incongruities. As surprising as the total docility with which, in his early years, he made brilliant copies of the works of Delacroix, Carpaccio and Poussin is the depth of his refusal to admit any common ground between himself and other masters. The success of his endeavour is marred by moments of frustration: a friend told Edmond de Goncourt that she had witnessed Moreau screaming with rage at his mother when they were both on holiday in Honfleur, and one of his pupils reports him as ranting on at him for a full twenty minutes. By the same token he made private and acid notes on his friend Fromentin's interpretation of Rembrandt in *Les Maîtres d'autrefois*, while the Musée Gustave Moreau contains watercolours alarming in their formless and bloody outpourings. The mightiness of his effort to control his world is reflected in the commentaries which Moreau wrote on his paintings. Perfervid, hallucinatory, onanistic, these are designed to repel the intruder as much as to protect the image.

For as secret worlds go, Moreau's is fairly accessible, peopled as it is with the stock paraphernalia of mythology and theology, although characters as familiar as Hercules, Jason, Oedipus, Orestes, Orpheus, Jacob, Moses, David and Christ have undergone such a profound change that they all appear to be intimately related. The unifying factor is that sort of lymphatic trance which Moreau called "*la belle Inertie*". Inertia was to him neither a fateful nor a voluptuous quality; it was, rather, a wise substitute for passion. Inertia strikes Oedipus into thoughtful immobility, while the Sphinx claws at his chest; Prometheus dreams with the rapt attention of the self-absorbed while the eagle extracts his liver; Jason, about to clasp the Golden Fleece, pauses with his foot on the monster, while Medea lays a pallid hand on his shoulder; and Hercules, pictured on the night when he impregnated the fifty daughters of Thespius, remains motionless and uninvolved, because, according to Moreau, he feels the immense sadness of the creator. These sleepwalkers, stylistically rooted in the outlines of Mantegna and Sodoma, and the *morbidezza* of Luini, are supplemented by their counterparts, a procession of gracile female nudes, adolescents loaded with arcane jewellery, which, according to another of his maxims, represents *"la Richesse nécessaire"*. These women, who become progressively more menacing, owe something to both Cranach and Crivelli.

The plot, in all cases, centres on the attempt of the seductive female to corrupt and debase the innocent dreaming male, and the execution rarely stands up to the weight of malefic intention. Debauchery, it is understood, leads to death, and the debauchery is always imposed by a woman, never undertaken voluntarily by a man. Occasionally, as in the late *Jupiter and Semele*, the painter's state of mind seems to verge on insanity, possibly because the subject of the picture involves the revenge of the male figure. Semele died when she entreated Jupiter to appear to her as a god, and was unable to bear the sight of his majesty. In Moreau's picture the gigantic deity, encrusted with jewels, and bearing a pink lotus, is impervious to the small creature slithering from his embossed knee. His eyes have a heavily outlined iconic fixity, which indicates Hindu sources. Accretions of decorative detail adhere to every surface. It is a truly alarming manifestation.

In all these works a penumbra of genuine mystery is added by the elaboration of extraordinary hybrid architectural and atmospheric backgrounds which are extremely impressive. There is sufficient evidence in the form of early watercolours to suggest that had Moreau not succumbed to or been overtaken by the Romantic agony – which sees the embattled artist besieged on all sides by the perverse and

destructive temptations of women with burning eyes and cold hearts
– he would have been a first-class minor landscape painter. This,
however, would have disappointed a great many people.

For Moreau was treasured above all by men of letters. To them he
was one who gave appearance to their convictions and a recognizable
décor to their world, a world dominated by anxiety, mistrust and
premonition. The lubricious reactions of his contemporaries to his
images of sinless sinning reflect very faithfully the delight that
Flaubert took in detailing the attractions of Salammbô or the tempt-
ing of St Anthony, while the intrusion of Eastern mysteries into those
properly pertaining to Greece or Judaea is analogous to the eclectic
and basically irreligious credo of Leconte de Lisle. This second *mal du
siècle* deserves a firmer dating and a less lyrical blanket coverage.
Like sufferers from the earlier malady, this exhausted generation
compensated most powerfully for the vitiating effects of reading
Schopenhauer by a scrupulous artistic performance. This, characteristically, involved effort, pain, and a durability of form that did duty
for personal redemption. It was inevitable that Moreau, who was an
avid reader of Banville, Gautier, Baudelaire and Flaubert, should be
conscripted into this contemporary Parnassus.

Painters, however, disposed of him far more briskly. Manet and
Degas both considered him something of a fraud; Renoir unkindly
remarked that he exaggerated the precious colours and the gold leaf in
order to appeal to Jewish collectors. For the astonishing thing about
Moreau's career is that most of it was contemporary with the birth
and maturity of Impressionism. Perhaps he supplied a quality that the
Impressionists lacked: high finish. Zola, torn between his loyalty to his
Impressionist friends and his own predilections as a collector of high-
priced junk, found himself in a difficult position when reviewing
Moreau's pictures in the Salons of 1876 and 1878. He was shocked by
what he considered to be the retrograde nature of Moreau's art, and
disarmed by the sheer quality of the bric-à-brac. He falls into the

writer's trap of animating the scene with sounds and scents; then, pulling himself together with an effort, announces that the final effect of Moreau's pictures is to make him want to paint the first slut he sees in the street.

M. Mathieu has been working on Moreau for many years; it is interesting to find even a contemporary scholar falling prey to the temptation of description that has afflicted all previous writers on Moreau, and omitting essential data, such as a full list of the volumes in Moreau's library. To keep the temperature high, Moreau's incantations must be retained, if only as a contrast – or perhaps a comparison – with the large but curiously weightless images that they accompanied. It is only in this way that one can decide whether there is more or less to Moreau than meets the eye.

12

Ploughing a Provincial Furrow *

ABROAD, IN PROVINCIAL CITIES, indolent and homesick, one turns, as ever, to the museum. When one is in this mood great masterpieces no longer serve their purpose: they are too important, too strenuous; they belong to a world outside one's own. From long experience one learns to follow the arrow which says *Ecole française XIXe. siècle*, and there on the attic floor, ignored by a somnolent attendant, are those faithful and sturdy mediocrities whose confidence, unattenuated by years of public neglect, will somehow shoulder one through until teatime. Jules Dupré, Léon Cogniet, Felix Ziem, Rosa Bonheur: no artistic claims can be made for them. Their terrible colours, glistening *craquelure*, instant respectability, infinite tedium, represent some ancient moment of repose, before the long march of modern art was to begin. They match one's nostalgia for simple rules, simple illustrations, simple nourishment. But of course such things were never simple; they were at all times complex and sad.

Nostalgia for idealized simplicity is one of the oldest vices of a civilized society. Scholars in America are turning from Manet to Gérôme, from Cézanne to Decamps, from Gauguin to Rosa Bonheur. There are many spurious justifications for such scholarly activity. One might, for example, argue that there are no up-to-date standard works, that one cannot ignore public taste, that the time has come for such

*Dore Ashton and Denise Browne Hare, *Rosa Bonheur. A Life and a Legend*. Secker & Warburg. *The Times Literary Supplement*, 16 October 1981.

artists to be rediscovered. Visitors to the Second Empire exhibition at the Grand Palais in 1979, where crowds gazed in wonder at the portraits of Winterhalter, nevertheless found that such works had no staying power. Elevated to a rank to which they could never have aspired in their lifetime, the Dubufes and the Coutures and the Detailles failed to make their mark. They do better in the dusty corridors of provincial museums, those Père Lachaises of the respectably dead, the harmless, the unassuming, the forgotten. There, on the appropriate afternoon, the traveller, his timespan rendered infinite by the absence of familiar landmarks, may savour for a while the beguiling and misleading placidity of certain areas of the nineteenth century.

I hesitate to "research" how many PhD students there are at present tunnelling down these byways, although an hour with a computer would reveal all. I remember that last year Professor Albert Boime devoted 683 pages to Thomas Couture, and that his book was a very handsome production: the artist, however, remains unvisited. In the same year Horace Vernet was given an exhibition in Rome and Ary Scheffer one in Paris; on reflection they were revealed as rather worse than one remembered them. Oscar Wilde warned that the only person who could appreciate all works of art was an auctioneer. We would do well to recognize the separateness of our love of images and our longing for a past we never knew. They are not the same.

In the meantime, Rosa Bonheur, horse painter *extraordinaire*, has been honoured with a biography, the first for seventy years. In addition to being a painter of international, if ephemeral, repute, she was a liberated woman, although whether she thought so herself is another matter and no doubt belongs in another book. Dore Ashton is too good an art historian, and, to judge by the illustrations in the present volume, Denise Browne Hare too good a photographer to try to mediate the truth here, namely that Rosa Bonheur, who painted perhaps two pictures of renown, *The Horse Fair* and *Ploughing in the Nivernais*, is mainly remembered for the fact that she dressed as a man, that she formed a lesbian *ménage* with Nathalie Micas, and after the latter's death with Anne Elizabeth Klumpke, that she bought and lived in a potentially exquisite manor house on the edge of the forest of Fontainebleau which she transformed into a menagerie, heads of stuffed elk and reindeer thrusting out from the walls of the salon to contemplate the collection of goats, horses, forty sheep, two lions, innumerable dogs and a yak, all of which were encouraged to wander through the house. Over this domain Rosa Bonheur reigned supreme, her impressive girth, short hair, and bluff senatorial features well-known in the vicinity and apparently accepted without criticism. While she drew and painted her animals, and occasionally shot them, Nathalie Micas rested from her household labours by inventing a new type of brake for a steam engine. This she was unable to test, and it can be assumed to have failed.

Rosa Bonheur was one of the unfortunate children of Raimond Bonheur, painter and enthusiast, and of his wife Sophie. On his arrival in Paris in 1828 Raimond Bonheur became enraptured by the ideal of universal brotherhood then being propagated by the Saint-Simonians, and, dedicating himself to the betterment of humanity, he left his wife to support the family by taking in needlework. He seems to have been a madman, drunk on the empty words and gestures put about by Enfantin and becoming a member of his monastery at Ménilmontant, where his wife and children were permitted to visit him, until it was closed down by the government. Raimond Bonheur was also a tearful man with a penchant for dressing up: the child Rosa was frequently accoutred as a Templar, and Corot painted her wearing a large plumed hat with her infant smock. After Sophie Bonheur had wasted away and died, Rosa Bonheur, wisely in the circumstances, decided to transfer her affections to the animal kingdom. Trained in the rudiments of drawing by her father, and possibly stimulated by the lectures of Geoffroy de Saint Hilaire, who stressed that anatomical organisms are basically analogous, any differences being metamorphic variations of an original type or pattern, Rosa donned breeches and a painter's jacket, and, after a brief period of copying in the Louvre, went to study her special subject in the abbatoirs and horse fairs of Paris and its environs and at the dissecting benches in her father's studio. She began to exhibit in the Salon of 1840, when she was nineteen, and from that moment was very successful, enjoying her greatest acclaim with *The Horse Fair* of 1853, a five-metre-long canvas now in the Metropolitan Museum in New York and described latterly by John Rewald as "a majestic exercise in futile dexterity".

It does not in fact wear too badly. It is based on a composition by Horace Vernet of 1827, which is in its turn based on Géricault's studies for *The Riderless Horse Race* of 1817, which in their turn derive from the casts of the Parthenon frieze made by the sculptor Giraud in London and kept in his studio in Rome. By the time the pattern has come to rest with Rosa Bonheur, a certain Second Empire domestication has set in: the horses are percherons, they trot rather than rear, and the horse traders are kitted out in caps and waistcoats and full moustaches. Yet the heroic element is still there, helped out in this instance by those haphazard features that sometimes make a composition memorable: a diagonal barrier of trees, a patterning of patches of blue across the canvas, and a foreground of dusty cobbles made to resemble those of Géricault, i.e. tremulous, as of milk coming to the boil.

This is the only picture by Rosa Bonheur which takes cognizance of any other picture. The rest of the time she is happy with her droves of animals, sometimes portrayed as part of the labourer's lot, but more often depicted in a world of their own. It could perhaps be said that there is some sort of analogy between her picture of *Ploughing in the Nivernais*, pietist, quietist, every clod of earth hectically lit, and the novels of Champfleury. It is better, however, not to make cross-cultural claims for her. The only sign she gives of attending to the life of her times is her enthusiasm for the Wild West and Red Indian spectacle brought to Paris by Buffalo Bill Cody, a sell-out success which she commemorated by painting a portrait of Buffalo Bill himself. Although famous in France, America and England, and enjoying the favour of both Queen Victoria and Empress Eugénie, she had no vitality as an artist, and her hard-edged technique soon deteriorated into a hesitant and smudged parody of her earlier style. She became very rich and was content to rest on her laurels, gained so early and at such cost. She did not care much about painting, but was proud to be famous as a painter.

Her reputation was indeed very great, although this is reflected mainly in the prices her works fetched rather than in the critical eulogies of her contemporaries. The debates concerning Realism and Impressionism could hardly include her; she remains as one of those mid-century phenomena who are themselves their own best advertisement, and although it cannot be said that she conformed to everyone's idea of a successful artist, she had certain revered artistic appurtenances, notably a reputation for singularity and a wildly picturesque and elaborate studio setting. Her sexual preferences attracted not a whisper of blame, and although Germaine Greer advances the theory that her domestic arrangements provide the only context in which a female artist could flourish, there seems little doubt that Rosa Bonheur would have painted animals – to destruction, if necessary – whatever her entourage, and that she would have painted them just as well, or as badly, as her public wanted her to. Money, not sex, seems to have been the enabling factor in her case. Once she could afford her château and her menagerie, her artistic efforts slackened, and she was quite happy never to learn another thing. She seems to have felt a late passion for Anne Elizabeth Klumpke, to whom she left her entire estate; no obstacles were put in her way, and they painted terrible pictures together, in perfect harmony.

Rosa Bonheur was in a sense out of the feminist debate for she never pretended to be a woman, never claimed any glories for her sex, or let it be known that she was engaged in any kind of struggle. She recognized (and this is a genuine trait of greatness) no enemies. She was on excellent terms with her dealers, her patrons and her friends: once she had mastered the rudiments of court etiquette she was as easily at home with the Empress Eugénie as with Buffalo Bill. It was probably predestined that she could only operate on her own singular terms, and if these consisted of cross-dressing and encouraging lions to roam up and down her staircase she considered these activities to be perfectly normal. She expressed deep pleasure in the beauties of the forest of Fontainebleau, and although undeniably stricken by the death of Nathalie Micas, there is no evidence that she suffered from doubt, despair, crises of identity, or other fashionable ills endured by both women and men. Of her luxurious maturity there is evidence in the evocative photographs that illustrate the book. Of her bizarre beginnings there may be another story to be told, but Rosa Bonheur did not choose to tell it.

It is interesting to compare Professor Ashton's carefully non-committal account of her life with that of Theodore Stanton (*Reminiscences of Rosa Bonheur*, Andrew Melrose, 1910), which garners all the available evidence about her from her friends and relations still living, and also starts a number of hares which Professor Ashton has thought it wise not to pursue. The most striking feature of Stanton's very long monograph is the sheer absence of sexual patronage, of sexual propaganda, of sexual curiosity. It seems, amazingly enough, that in 1910 the spectacle of a woman dressing as a man and living with another woman aroused not a whisper of scandal and was accepted as a feature of the landscape in a manner so calm that today's feminists appear in the guise of Don Quixote in comparison. Stanton suggests that the climate of opinion had been thoroughly prepared by the Saint-Simonians, who visualized the Deity as both male and female (*"Faisons régner notre Dieu, Père et Mère"*) and were waiting for a lady Messiah to emerge from the surrounding spiritual chaos to effect a

mystic marriage with Enfantin, the leader of the sect. For a time
George Sand was tipped as the most likely candidate, although she
made it clear that she did not care for the honour. There was also a
certain ambiguity about the Saint-Simonians' formal dress; the men
wore tight bodices which had to be laced up the back by a colleague,
and the women a sort of early cycling outfit, consisting of a skirt worn
over trousers. From that position to the acceptance of a woman in
trousers is but a step, especially if that woman behaves like a man and
signs her letters, *"Votre vieille culotte de peau de général"*. The enormous
prestige of George Sand herself may have blurred the distinction.

Stanton's other interesting point is that Rosa Bonheur was
completely philistine. Decorated by the King of Spain and the
Emperor of Mexico, Officer of the Legion of Honour, a hot property
in America, she appears to have lived unaware of the existence of the
Barbizon school practically on her doorstep. She was, literally, uninter-
ested in everything except the depiction of animals. Her numerous
letters to her friends and family are hearty, artless, full of joke names
and phrases, misspelt, and totally lacking in information. There is one
solitary gleam of spite directed at Jules de Goncourt, whom she met at
a dinner; the Goncourts retaliated by describing her as a hideous low-
born Polish Jew in their *Journal*. One feels that however taxing Rosa
Bonheur may have been in private life she kept her head well above the
poisonous waters of literary and artistic gossip, and that in maintain-
ing her extremely limited but not unhealthy outlook on life she may in
fact have been a rather admirable figure.

But as a painter she still belongs to the indolent afternoon in the
provincial museum, or perhaps to a rather more steadfast pilgrimage
to the village of Thoméry and to her Château de By. Few would spare
a glance at her canvases on a visit to Fontainebleau. Anne Elizabeth
Klumpke, in what can only be assumed to be her innocence, donated
her vast Rosa Bonheur holdings to the château in 1929, thinking them
no doubt able to survive the same scrutiny as the Primaticcio gallery

and Napoleon's throne room. The Bonheur galleries have been closed for many years now, a state of affairs which would have been unimaginable to the *New York Herald's* Paris correspondent for 31 May 1900. "Rosa Bonheur studio sale," he reported. "Proceeds of the first day amount to more than half a million francs. OXEN MOST IN DEMAND. Stags also fetch very high prices."

13

The Willing Victim *

CLOWNS DO NOT MAKE one laugh. Undersized, deliberately grotesque, on the verge of tears, they induce discomfort. Their function is to be humiliated, by powerful men and pretty girls, aided and abetted by the audience, and the process by which this is accomplished is a diabolical set-piece of collusion. Clowns are also held to be asexual (though lovesick), innocent, and on the side of the good: they are frequently photographed for the newspapers with their arms round a couple of children, or heard on early morning radio programmes promoting campaigns for road safety.

We are supposed to identify with clowns because they appeal to the undersized innocents we all know ourselves to be. I suspect this process to be abominable. The undying popularity of Buster Keaton and Charlie Chaplin, particularly with the not so young, points up another parallel: when we are not being undersized and innocent we are being dignified and misunderstood. This is a stance we take up at our peril, and if we do so we must realize that we are acting out of a mistimed and misplaced romanticism. Let it not be forgotten that clowns are also wreckers, that they kick women, ruin machinery, and spill buckets of nameless substances over and over again on the public highway. They confuse and exhaust those who attempt to control or organize them, they win the affections of the pretty girl, who takes

*Robert F. Storey, *Pierrot: A Critical History of a Mask*. Princeton University Press. *The Times Literary Supplement*, 21 December 1979.

pity on them, and they never learn. Why should they? Their technique has been described, in another context, as winning by losing. It is not to be emulated.

At his most acceptable the clown is Pierrot, a white-faced archetype with a distinguished and slightly mysterious pedigree, consistently promoted by Romantics in one age or another as a synonym for the hapless and the unassimilated. This character is not a creation of the nineteenth century but of the rational eighteenth, and although the many lowly comedians who brought this supporting role to life have long been forgotten, the pictures by means of which he was presented to the people have not.

In the introduction to this book, the early chapters of which are crammed with excellent information, Robert F. Storey declines to take the fine arts as evidence, and he is probably wise, for the evidence is largely a cover for the artist's own isolation. Whether this identification is valid or not belongs inside another book. There is, however, a small amount of documentary material which throws light on the historical function of Pierrot and at the same time on his mutation into the semi-sacred figure he was to become.

Pierrot was of course Italian and became naturalized into French. As Pedrolino he was one of the less important servants in the Commedia dell'Arte, stupid but quick on his feet. He appears to have been an object of rivalry between the Italian players, who had a devoted following in Paris in the second half of the seventeenth century, and Molière's company, playing to equally packed houses at the Hôtel de Bourgogne. Molière, not a man to ignore the achievements of his rivals, took him over and presented him as Pierre ("Pierrot" being a diminutive) in his *Don Juan, ou le festin de Pierre* in 1665.

With Molière the transformation into the slacker, more indulgent character begins to get under way: Pierrot is a slow-witted and lovelorn peasant who speaks dialect and probably wears the traditional white smock of the country yokel. In 1673 the Italians took this character back, called him Pietro, and kept him dull and in love; he was a subordinate character until played by a comic of genius called Giaratone. It would seem from this man's performances that we can date the rise of Pierrot and the decline of the first comedian, Harlequin. In 1684 Giaratone appeared as Pierrot in *Arlequin, empereur dans la lune*. In the same year the painter Watteau was born in Valenciennes. When he arrived in Paris he was already at work as a theatre designer and was later to paint a drop curtain for *Arlequin, empereur dans la lune*. It was Watteau's lifelong fascination with the masks and characters of the Théâtre Italien that gave a peculiar and perhaps misleading resonance to his own fantasies.

But it is necessary to remember Pierrot's alternative function. This tongue-tied innocent refined by the power of love is also a casual and quick-witted *farceur*. He makes his public work for him, a function that audiences were forced to assume when small French troupes, setting up in imitation of the Italians in the two main Paris fairs, were forbidden to use dialogue. Huge placards bearing their verses were introduced onto the trestle stages and the players mimed while the delighted audience sang their words to the tunes of popular songs. The nimble professionalism of the players seems to have been their most attractive attribute, and it was probably this aspect of their lives that most beguiled Claude Gillot, Watteau's master, and Watteau himself.

Gillot's bleak little pictures, particularly the *Two Carriages* in the Louvre, remind us of the bashing and swiping aspects of the performances, too often obscured by the moonlit stillness laid over the subject by the Symbolists and the Decadents. In Gillot's picture a furious altercation is being waged between two valets, dressed *à la française*. In the sedan chairs of their respective masters a further and equally undignified argument is taking place, but here the characters are masked, in *travesti*, and wearing exaggerated headgear. A dignified cleric, perhaps a vestigial descendant of one of Molière's *raisonneurs*, attempts to intercede. The background is an entirely sober town square, whose rational and even classical architecture acts as a mute comment to the nose-to-nose clenched fist fury of the protagonists.

Gillot's picture gives an impression of concerted effort, and Watteau's reaction to this ideal troupe, into which the cloddish and unfortunate Pierrot could, in the last scene, be reassimilated, was predictable. A sick man, Watteau was the first to identify himself with Pierrot, not overtly, but with beguiling subtlety. In the Edinburgh *Fêtes vénitiennes* the haggard player of the bagpipes, with his yearning face and loose white collar, plays for the heroine. She dances opposite a fat man in oriental costume, a Sultan figure; she is very young and spreads her satin skirts with ceremony. In the background a man in a tremendous tricorne hat strides away in a fit of pique. The love of Léandre for Isabelle, the courtship of the amorous Doctor, and the hopeless wooing of Pierrot, his servant, have given cohesion to what is perhaps an autobiographical statement.

The Italian Commedia, high-spirited and cruel, relying on virtuoso individual improvisations on stock situations within a fairly skeletal framework, might well provide the key to the inspiration of Watteau's art and to its iconography. But there are signs that Watteau, like one of the players, made his own improvisations. The operation of fantasy transformed the theatre of fact; the personal nostalgia of the artist turned a popular number into an apotheosis. Moreover, like an impresario, Watteau takes liberties with costume and character. The highly traditional clothes of the Commedia players become slightly more languorous and aristocratic as Watteau grafts on to them the wider ruffs and the richer satins to be found in those pictures by Rubens which he was able to study in the Luxembourg. Then, having re-clothed his characters, and given them far more distinction than they originally possessed, he isolates them, relegating to the background those for whom he feels no particular interest.

Thus Pantaloon and the Doctor, staple props of any Commedia performance, make only a brief appearance on the extreme edge of

Watteau's pictures. Isabelle is permanently separated from her lover, and even Harlequin is overshadowed by the two minor characters for whom Watteau reserves his most intense feelings: Mezzetin and Pierrot. Mezzetin, the wily companion of Harlequin, has become a fastidious commentator, idealistic and at the same time disabused. Pierrot, the simplest and most obscure member of the company, is given quasi-tragic status, the status of the *Pierrot lunaire* beloved of the nineteenth century.

To be a member of the troupe was Watteau's abiding wish, if not Pierrot's. In *L'Amour au théâtre italien* Watteau gives us his ideal metaphor: a collection of strolling players, casually in love on a summer night, lit by the flares of torches. Here Pierrot occupies a position just to the left of centre; he wears the traditional white *casaque* and trousers, white ruff and round hat, and he plays the guitar. It is interesting to note that he obscures Harlequin, a slightly ominous figure in his black mask and diamond-patterned costume. Pierrot is becoming the force that brings the troupe together.

In a later picture, painted in London as payment to the celebrated Dr Mead, whom Watteau had travelled to consult about his fatal illness, the Italian players fan out brilliantly from the central figure of Pierrot, who stands quite still and bolt upright. He looks triumphant, breathless, and secretive. He has just performed a somersault, perhaps, or some more arcane magic, for the composition is based on one of the many available representations of the Ecce Homo, or Christ shown to the people. The fact that Léandre "introduces" the character to the audience, points him out with exaggerated respect, and the rest of the troupe talk, grimace, or mime throughout this presentation, gives weight to the hypothesis.

The Pierrot as Man of Sorrows simile was first propounded by Dora Panofsky with regard to Watteau's most famous picture, the *Gilles*. Gilles was a generic name used by French versions of this honest but stupid pander and clown, and probably derived from a

mid-seventeenth-century comedian and acrobat who called himself
Gilles le Niais. From Watteau's extraordinary, and extraordinarily
large picture, we can almost reconstruct a typical pantomime or
parade. Attempts are made to drive some sense into the head of Gilles
le Niais (who is not yet wearing white make-up). He is given a dancing-
master, a drawing-master, a fencing-master: all to no avail. At this
point a donkey is led across the stage to underline his ineffable
stupidity. This is the moment painted by Watteau. The proportions of
the picture, and its low viewpoint, which makes the coral ribbons on
the shoes the correct focus for the eye, indicates that this was a theatre
billboard, propped up on the trestle stage to entice the passers-by in
to a performance. The fact that Gilles or Pierrot is chosen as the
supremely important character of the troupe proves what literary
evidence has failed to do: that the Romantic isolation of Pierrot dates
from 1721.

For this reason later avatars of Pierrot decline in importance,
although, as was to be expected, the character became heroic in
the nineteenth century. While the giant platitudes of *Hernani* and
Chatterton were being thundered out of the Théâtre Français,
the alternative theatre was playing to appreciative audiences in the
Funambules. The attraction was Baptiste Deburau, who powdered
his face white, blackened his eyebrows, and reddened his lips; the ruff
was removed and the loose white head-covering replaced by a black
skull-cap. This angry pthisic Pierrot was both violent and sinister, with
something of a self-conscious professional's spleen. It is no accident
that in the 1840s Daumier draws Pierrot, now metamorphosed into
the more universal *saltimbanque*, as a shabby, embittered, and by no
means young man, surrounded by his family, and striding grimly off to
the next pitch.

The two final transformations were both effected in the nineteenth
century, and both obtain today. The first is the legacy of Paul Legrand,
an actor who had formerly played Léandre, and who brought to the

part of Pierrot the sensitivity of a lover. In *Les Enfants du paradis* Jean-Louis Barrault may have been closer to Legrand than to Debureau. The second mutation was brought about by Paul Margueritte, who, in 1881, wrote a *Pierrot assassin de sa femme*, in which the main character tickles Columbine's feet until she dies laughing. The subversive and extremely frightening import of this little play should be retained by all those in danger of succumbing to the theory that Pierrot is a character of heroic stature. It is ironic to note that this sentimental view obliterates all others throughout the brutal twentieth century.

Professor Storey's book is a welcome addition to the literature of the Commedia dell'Arte, for which the main texts are Luigi Riccoboni's *Histoire du théâtre italien*, published in 1730, and Allardyce Nicoll's *The World of Harlequin: A Critical Study of the Commedia dell'Arte*, published in 1963. The author is perhaps a little too selective. At some point he diverges from his excellent main theme to follow the fortunes of Pierrot in the poetry of T.S. Eliot and Wallace Stevens. This is unconvincing, and a study of Banville and Verlaine would have been more appropriate. Pierrot as metaphor is an easy option; Pierrot as a fate to be endured is far more difficult to contemplate.

14

Descent into the Untestable *

THOSE WHO ARE UNWILLING or unable to accept the fact that the wicked flourish like the green bay tree, and who seek to identify some original fault which may account for this distressing phenomenon, more keenly evident in the twentieth century than in any other, will delight in the thesis put forward by Robert Harbison in this badly produced, badly written, and undeniably brilliant book. But first of all, those to whom the book will be meat and drink must accept the fact that it is written at two distinct turns of speed. The preface, which lays down the main argument, gives the impression of having been set forth in all its innocent pugnacity as a synopsis for an interested editor, or as an application for a scholarship, or both. The text itself, which purports to illustrate the points made in the preface, appears to have been written some years later, for the style, which veers from the crepuscular to the opaque, is different, and the argument alternately tenses and sags under the weight of the complicated centuries whose progression – or regression – the author chronicles. It is to Mr Harbison's great credit that he manages to sum himself up at the end. But in his end is not quite his beginning.

It is Mr Harbison's contention that in the eighteenth century certain painters and writers inaugurated a deliberate regression, presumably away from reason and the testing of hypotheses, in favour of those

*Robert Harbison, *Deliberate Regression*. André Deutsch. *The Times Literary Supplement*, 17 October 1980.

areas of consciousness which cannot be tested: the making of new myths, whose outcome would be a new transcendence. This enterprise, which after disparate beginnings gained strength and adherents, came to be known as the Romantic Movement, in which, it was hoped, ways round or even out of the dilemma of consciousness would be found in primitivism, pantheism, and the insidious detachment of meaning from image or sound or word. Ultimately, the original significance of such images and words would be lost, hypotheses would no longer be tested, or susceptible to the process of testing, and the desire for transcendence, which is permanent and endemic to the human species, could be manipulated and attached to more useful concepts.

Mr Harbison simplifies and strengthens his argument by basing it on certain pre-selected works of art, although he omits a great many examples which might point in the opposite direction. If one follows his line of thinking it will seem obvious that Neoclassicism is responsible for the Third Reich, that the festivals of the Revolution of 1789 provided the inspiration for the Nuremberg rallies and the heroic, unfocused, and over-lifesized statues of Soviet workers armed with hammers and sickles, instruments which would surely be obsolete in the collectivist millennium.

It is an argument familiar to most critics of Romanticism. But Mr Harbison's theme of regression, which he states without any reference to psychoanalytical theory, enables him to cast his nets wider. He differs from the normal run of historians by pronouncing the anathema rather earlier than one would expect. He starts, in fact, with Watteau, whose fantasies he finds deeply sinister, and along with Watteau he indicts his pupil, Boucher, and his disciple, Fragonard, two painters of a very different stamp, who translated Watteau's original idiom into a lazy repetition of shorthand patterns for youth and irresponsibility.

This descent into infantilism, says Mr Harbison, is where it all began to go wrong. But even those who doubt the ability of Watteau,

Boucher and Fragonard to influence the main currents of European thinking will surely note the differences, as opposed to the similarities, in their styles. Watteau, low-born, tubercular, a drifter from Flanders, had been denied access to the main traditions of mythological and allegorical painting by the very paucity of his training; he was therefore predisposed to accept the idiom with which he was presented by his masters Gillot and Audran, out of which he fashioned a fairly melancholy world of high-class nomads, slightly overdressed, in settings visibly adapted from stage backdrops. The young pouting faces to which Mr Harbison objects are more noticeable in the paintings than in the drawings because Watteau was a better draughtsman than he was a painter. A drawing of a woman's face by Watteau will display signs of weary middle age, which, when translated onto canvas by his notoriously dirty brush, will become blank and doll-like.

Boucher, it is true, shows a tendency to see his characters as about fourteen years old, but even this tendency derived from Watteau's reductions, for Boucher was one of the artists employed to engrave Watteau's entire work, and in the process of engraving the original subtleties became mechanized to a far more considerable degree. It should also be remembered that Boucher had a deep dislike of nature and refused to work from the model. His extreme facility with the brush appealed to Fragonard, more truly gifted, more capable of ardour, and when Fragonard became Boucher's pupil he adopted his idiom uncritically. It is true that there are corrupt elements in Fragonard, but not enough to make him bear the weight of subsequent history.

The only significant error (error being the eighteenth-century equivalent of Mr Harbison's regression) propagated by the age of reason arose out of the need to provide a secular alternative for good-hearted and right-thinking non-believers: the myth of the excellence of the classical past. This was largely the creation of Winckelmann, who pleaded his cause in terms so incantatory that some of his arguments remain persuasive to this day. For Winckelmann the ancient world was a repository of wise laws, good government, and, above all, physical beauty. Greece was peopled by athletes seven feet tall, marble-white, and generally adolescent. There were no women. Ancient Rome was thought to be a city of bleached white fragments, although in its heyday it must have looked rather more like the Oxford Street façade of Selfridges. The inhabitants of such cities and their provinces were thought to possess the secrets of living beautifully and dying well, propositions overwhelmingly attractive to those without faith in the supernatural. Winckelmann's error was to persuade himself that one might possess those secrets by "imitating" the ways of the Greeks and the Romans as perceived through their artefacts and by trying to resemble them as closely as possible.

To persuade himself was not difficult; when it came to persuading others Winckelmann's system, while retaining a remarkable surface unity, became deeply flawed by the residual beliefs and disobedient energies of its various proponents. David's *Oath of the Horatii* and *Death of Socrates*, which are cited, represent the only moment of stasis, achieved by a purely secular, physical and masculine ethic in an attempt to abolish the laxness, self-indulgence and feminization of artistic symbols brought about by those very artists whom Mr Harbison has already castigated. The style of the *Horatii* can be labelled fascist (and has), but only if it is possible to discount David's own fantasies of strength and steadfastness, qualities which he himself did not possess. Nevertheless, Neoclassical agitprop can be seen to have influenced the behaviour of certain extremists during the Revolution of 1789, as well as the physical appearance of its festivals.

But if the eighteenth century was when it all went wrong, Mr Harbison omits to say that this was the last time when it might just have come out right. To leave out of one's calculations Montesquieu and Diderot, neither of them afflicted with any beliefs they could not verify, and to weight the argument instead with Fragonard,

Winckelmann and David, is to misunderstand the limitations of art. Artistic traditions are self-generating and at best reflexive. One cannot live by the light of ideas expressed in pictures, although their images will colour one's thinking. A painter can give us an image of old age which will capture the poignancy of faded eyes and seamed flesh, but a painter will not be able to pass on the kind of last message left by Montesquieu: that if he were to be given his time again he would concentrate on keeping warm in the winter and eating ices in the summer. Quite simply, a different kind of information is being imparted. Pictures occasionally need the corroboration of the written word, which Mr Harbison is willing to supply in the nineteenth and twentieth centuries but not to any great extent in the eighteenth.

Indeed if the painted evidence demonstrates one kind of truth about the eighteenth century, it must be stated that the written evidence demonstrates quite another. In 1756 Mme du Deffand wrote to Voltaire, *"Monsieur de Voltaire, vous combattez et détruisez toutes les erreurs, mais que mettez-vous à leur place?"* She meant that once Voltaire had shown that religion was erroneous (or regressive) there would be no opportunity for her to use those faculties which could only be satisfied by pious observance and the need for belief, however irrational. The dangers of reason were also noted by La Mettrie in his treatise *De la Folie*: *"On arrive à constater que plus on gagnera du côté de l'esprit, plus on perdra du côté de l'instinct."* Reason and emotion, the two polarities by which the eighteenth century measured its progress – and both were thought to be equally useful – are abundantly evident in all the writings of Diderot, the tutelary genius of this particular argument.

By the same token it is a mistake to suppose, as Mr Harbison does, that David, in the *Oath of the Horatii*, is deficient in either one of these qualities. It is a passionate picture, but passionate in the sense in which Diderot's ideal actor is passionate: able to conceive of the role in a frenzy and to perform it with total control. The *Oath of the Horatii* certainly encapsulates a myth, but it is a myth about David himself, a myth of self-mastery. And although central to the European movement of Neoclassicism, it contains a myth which David himself was forced to abandon. While the painted image continues to exert its strength, the reality behind it is subject to change. That is what the picture does not and cannot tell us of its own accord.

For there is a truth even more terrible than Mr Harbison supposes, and it was discovered by certain members of the Romantic generation. The truth is this: reason does not work any better than myth, and will even produce its opposite. Eighteenth-century optimism was founded on the precept that reason would bring about change (for the better). The Revolution of 1789 was undertaken with this in mind. By 1791 the moment had passed. By 1793 it had become a nightmare, and David was painting *The Death of Marat* rather than more Horatii. The thinking men of Paris, friends and descendants of the *philosophes*, had somehow to accommodate the knowledge that a new method had been devised – by one of their own party, Collot d'Herbois – for disposing of opponents and nuisances: their live bodies could be tied to corpses and the whole parcel thrown into the river. Death would ensue, very slowly. This *noyade* was all the rage in Lyons, just as heads, with straw stuffed in their mouths and paraded on pikes, were a common sight in Paris. As Alfred de Musset said in 1836, "*Ne cherchez pas ailleurs le secret de nos maux.*"

Musset spoke for the generation denied the chance of fighting with and for Napoleon, the generation trained for a mythical future and condemned to an unsatisfactory present. The despair of the Romantics at the failure of both faith and reason is ignored by Mr Harbison, who prefers his regression unhampered by thought and finds it in the mythologies of Blake, Runge and Friedrich. He is confirmed in his beliefs, magnificently, by the outpourings of Ruskin and Wagner, both of whom were, by eighteenth-century standards, insane. In *De la folie*, La Mettrie lists, quite sympathetically, those attributes of madness which were to become a Romantic way of life:

melancholia, irritability, lassitude, alienation, a belief in the numinous, a tendency to vatic pronouncements. He describes this unhappy state as *"le délire sans fièvre"*. In the eighteenth century lunatics were thought to be the victims of bad luck. In the nineteenth century they were perceived as victims of history, and Mr Harbison might have cited Delacroix, who was fully aware of this dilemma, and who found all mythologies a cause for tragic rumination.

Indeed Mr Harbison weights his argument rather tendentiously by ignoring the main body of Romantic writings, by ignoring the attempts of those, like Baudelaire, who tried to fashion a new code of ethics out of the contemplation of works of art, a myth too insubstantial to succeed. Perversely he also ignores any *successful* Parnassian attempt to live by aesthetics alone. It is hardly fair, though undeniably persuasive, to concentrate on the Nazarenes and the Pre-Raphaelites, regressive to a man, without mentioning the Impressionists and their almost eighteenth-century delight in the here and now. Nor, to state the opposite case, would it be fair to discuss the Impressionist movement without noting the deliberate regression of the Fauves. But to indicate what has been left out is to demand another book, and that book, ideally, should be written by Mr Harbison himself. He is an important and useful commentator on a subject of enduring interest.

I cannot follow him any further, because my range is not so great as his. I think, however, that his argument dissolves, and that the attempt to create more myths becomes more threadbare, until we arrive at the bankruptcy of the Third Reich, which, ironically, is the only moment in history when the myth-making apparatus ever worked on a grand scale. I think he is unjust to William Morris, whose vision was far from laughable, that he concentrates too hard on Kandinsky, and not hard enough on Picasso, whose regression really is deliberate, and can be seen to be deliberate. I think he is wilful in avoiding the subject of abstract painting, into which one can read the significance of one's choice. But having inveighed against his style I must redress the balance and say that on many occasions his words are most marvellously right. Listening to Wagner, he experiences "a Gargantuan pulsation like seasickness". Reflecting on Kandinsky, he notes, "When the transformation of Kandinsky's pictures begins in 1909 the forms gradually lose their shapes, *like stewed fruit* [my italics]." He says of Burne-Jones, "He seeks a past without the trivial and reachable individuality of a year attached to it, like an address one could go to." He refers to "purplish Nürnberg". And I shall remember his beautiful phrase about "not-quite-relinquished hopes of transcendent coherence".

Mr Harbison supposes that we are living at the end of the world, and to judge by our present inability to create new myths he may be right. He is extremely angry about this and anxious to lay the blame on those who have failed to set the machine of history correctly, and have preferred the comfort of illusion and the sustaining mystery of faith. Like Alfred de Musset, he groans under the weight of a messed-up inheritance. But if myth-making leads to regression we may be in a healthier state than we suppose. If the Apocalypse is really just around the corner the correct attitude would seem to be one of lively curiosity. This would have been the attitude favoured in the eighteenth century. We might, in fact, sign off like Diderot, who believed in immortality of a kind: "*Vivant, j'agis et réagis en masse . . . mort, j'agis et réagis en molécules . . . Naître, vivre et passer, c'est changer de forme.*" We shall see. Or perhaps not, as the case may be.

15

Sick Servants of the Quill *

R OGER WILLIAMS, DISTINGUISHED professor in the Department
of History at the University of Wyoming, has drawn together,
under his Baudelairean title (but without its important corollary:
horreur de la vie, extase de la vie), five studies of nineteenth-century
French writers who have little in common apart from the fact that they
all died of an advanced venereal infection. Professor Williams's thesis,
if I understand him correctly, is that Baudelaire, Jules de Goncourt,
Flaubert, Maupassant, and Alphonse Daudet were unable to initiate or
sustain normal sexual relationships, had recourse to prostitutes, con-
tracted their infections, and concealed, obfuscated or dignified their
lamentable destinies behind the guise of dedication to the undifferenti-
ated ideal of Art, that great nineteenth-century alibi, the entity that
does not exist but which they called into being as the religious surrogate, the ultimate justification of their unlived lives, proclaiming that
without their particular afflictions they might not have given such great
service to literature. Edmond de Goncourt, in fact, put it about that his
brother died of fine writing, and the loyal and chaste Zola was chari-
table enough to believe him. Yet Daudet wondered if Flaubert's endless
search for the right word was not the result of his overdosing himself
with bromides which slowed his working tempo down to a frustrating
and protracted nightmare. There is room for argument on both sides.

*Roger L. Williams, *The Horror of Life*. Weidenfeld & Nicolson. *The Times Literary
Supplement*, 13 February 1981.

But first a word about Professor Williams, whose book is excellently written, profoundly disturbing, and strangely credulous. If Susan Sontag has written most movingly about illness as metaphor, Roger Williams has written about illness as illness, detailing with fascination, and apparent competence, the various states of mortal disease, with its grotesquely beautiful vocabulary, until the strange words build up an inevitability of their own, and the race towards the grave takes on an autonomy which, in its sinister way, is almost an art form in itself. It is actually a relief when death supervenes, when the funeral becomes a great literary apotheosis, and Zola, the only able-bodied man of letters left in France, re-enters as pall-bearer. The Romantic notion, which Professor Williams does not appear to endorse, is that life is so horrible that it is the artistic duty of a man of higher sensibility to spurn its vulgar attractions, to subvert its possibilities, and in general to get it over and done with, making as few concessions to normality as possible. "Art" (and the word is baleful in this context since it adds a spurious nobility to the process of avoiding Nature) will be the goal of the life-hater. Writing may thus be seen as a form of conversion hysteria.

But the story does not end there. *Chassez la Nature, elle revient au galop.* Tertiary syphilis, locomotor ataxia, epileptic convulsions, infantilism, premature death, were the price to be paid, and the return from Art to Nature was terrible indeed. In the last months of Jules de Goncourt's life Edmond was obliged to reprimand his adored and brilliant brother for dealing clumsily with his food in a restaurant, after which both men dissolved into tears before the astonished diners. *"Cré nom, cré nom"*, were the only words the stricken and aphasic Baudelaire could offer, and the nuns asked his mother to remove him from their hospital, as they could not tolerate blasphemy.

Professor Williams's method has been to scrutinize the letters and journals of the writers concerned, but not necessarily their formal published works, except in the case of Alphonse Daudet, whose *La*

Doulou chronicles his sufferings. The letters of Baudelaire, Flaubert and Maupassant are mainly concerned with their symptoms, which were horrifyingly numerous, their visits to various watering places, riverine establishments or warmer climates, in their search to obtain relief, their embarrassment of doctors (for they thought nothing of consulting seven or eight), and, last but by no means least, the financial burdens they were obliged to shoulder. The filiation of these themes is tenuous and obscure, and may even give rise to further diagnosis.

In the case of Baudelaire, Flaubert and Maupassant, the demands for or complaints about money are hysterical and obsessive, and have to do with their expectations from or responsibilities towards their mothers. Mme Baudelaire is punished in letters for having introduced her son to the horror of life, while Mmes Flaubert and Maupassant effectively restrict their sons in the same way, in case such sons should discover the ecstasy of life. And the need to write, and to justify themselves in the light of their mothers' disappointment, becomes a form of regression, paid for by a terrible simulacrum of marriage, in which both mother and son collude. By the same token, the writer's mistress, usually chosen for her unsuitability, viz. Baudelaire's illiterate mulatress Jeanne Duval, the Goncourts' shared Maria, a former midwife, and Maupassant's androgynous Gisèle, will serve one purpose only, but, if we are to believe Professor Williams, will not be allowed to serve it too well. Poor Louise Colet, who wanted love and conversation and a visit to Mme Flaubert, was looking entirely in the wrong direction.

It is easy to see how rapidly these authors become case histories, and how very possible it is to treat their lives as instances of inadequately realized sexuality, or morbid affliction, or disputed diagnosis, without at any point having to refer to their work as opposed to their tormented existence.

The position is further complicated by the fact that many doctors have been fascinated by the diseases of great men, and that it has been fashionable for medical experts to write their doctoral theses on the symptoms of a dead patient whom they have never once encountered. From the bibliography I select at random the following titles: "Gli 'attaques de nerfs' di Gustave Flaubert: Isterismo o epilessia?"; "Die Psychose Maupassants: Ein Kritischer Versuch", and "The last illness of Baudelaire", published in the *Urologic and Cutaneous Review* for 1934. As relatively recently as 1960 Dr Pierre Gallet asked, *"Quel diagnostique aurions-nous fait si nous avions soigné Flaubert?"* The one name left out of the bibliography is that of Oliver Sachs, yet it would seem that the latter's very beautiful style of writing may have influenced the way in which Professor Williams has set out his case studies. It can be stated with more certainty that he has paid closer attention to the medical than to the literary evidence, that this literary evidence is substantial, and that it ranges from the oblique testimony to sterility in Baudelaire's *Peintre de la vie moderne*, to the sanguinary fantasies manifested in *Salammbô* (which Flaubert preferred to *Madame Bovary*), to the novels of the brothers Goncourt, the most perfect accounts of failing health ever written, to the obsession with terrors and phobias that is inseparable from the style of Guy de Maupassant.

This brushing aside of the literary evidence can lead to a certain imbalance and indeed to a lack of judgement. Professor Williams states, of the brothers Goncourt, "We can sympathize with their indignation at the systematic incomprehension of their work, we can understand their consequent bitterness, we can even agree with many of their views; but we do not warm to them as beloved or admired writers." If this is indeed the case I suggest that we abandon the *Journal* for the novels and rediscover the delicacy and despair of Mme Gervaisais, who succumbs to the most terrible mental confusion in the heat of a Roman afternoon, of Soeur Philomène, who survives a kind of sexual death, and of Renée Mauperin, a modern girl who dies of a broken heart. That these stories work so brilliantly is due to the fact that the illness which in each case brings about the dénouement is used metaphorically, that illness is perceived as metaphor by these writers not only because they know about illness but because they know about metaphor. To confine sick writers to the symptoms of their disease may be fascinating, but it is not quite decent. There may be a terrible justice in Flaubert, high priest in the temple of Art, being downgraded to the subject of a learned article about the difference between hysterical and epileptic convulsions. But none of this quite explains *Madame Bovary*. Or, *pace* Professor Williams, *Madame Gervaisais*.

It is perhaps the nature of the illness from which these writers suffered, and which Professor Williams identifies as syphilis, that raises more questions than can be answered. At this point it might be pertinent to refer to an eighteenth-century manual written by an eminent doctor who was aware of the peculiar morbidity of the writing profession. Samuel-Auguste Tissot published his book, *De la santé des gens de lettres*, in Lausanne in 1768. He seems a sympathetic man, full of anecdotes, and apparently dedicated to the relief of the manifold ailments suffered by those chained to the quill. It becomes clear that practitioners of this craft do not undertake it without grave risk to their physical and mental stability. Dr Tissot, who is a bit of a gossip, describes two typical cases. *"L'on a vu un professeur de Berne, très versé dans la connaissance des langues orientales, homme encore dans la fleur de son age, et d'un travail infatigable, devenir imbécile et tomber en enfance."* Even more alarming is *". . . un jeune homme de famille, agé de 22 ans, s'étant livré jour et nuit à des études continues (et qui) tomba dans un délire qui devint bientôt phrénétique."* These two unfortunates could have passed quite easily into a nineteenth-century context, and might indeed have become the stuff of Romantic legend. The latter, in particular, might have been the subject of a short novel by Balzac.

Dr Tissot then itemizes the maladies to which men of letters are particularly prone: headaches, poor eyesight, muscular tension, diseases of the nervous system, palpitations, dizziness, lassitude, defective digestion, stupor, melancholia, gout, hair loss, tumours, aneurysms, ulcers, insomnia, apoplexy, constipation, flatulence, dropsy, impotence, isolation, *"des crachements incommodes"*, and, above all, *"la défiance, la crainte, la tristesse, l'abattement, le découragement"*. Most of this stems from sitting in one position for far too long, working in a bad light, breathing stale air, and, more important, neglecting the duties and pleasures of society.

So much for the diagnosis. Now the treatment. The first step is to get the patient to admit the error of his ways, and the doctor warns that because the man of letters tends to be cranky, intelligent, and obstinate, this may take some time, but it will be time well spent. Having made a full confession, the born-again writer is then in a position to observe a sensible regime.

He must take one or two hours of gentle exercise every day without fail. Dr Tissot recommends boating (Maupassant was not wrong), hunting, bowls, billiards or tennis. He must observe a rigorous diet, eschewing patés, custards, fritters, beans, and the more abstruse parts of certain animals. He may not eat more than two or at the most three dishes at each meal, and these should consist of poultry, fish, cereals, root vegetables, chicory, bread, milk, eggs and fruit. Permitted seasonings are sugar, salt, herbs, nutmeg and cinnamon. Cherries, an excellent dietary supplement, should be eaten between rather than after meals. Hot drinks are not encouraged, nor are coffee, chocolate, wine, tobacco, snuff, smoked meat and oil. The place of work should be in a salubrious neighbourhood, i.e. not near tanneries, abattoirs, or butchers' shops. The head should be kept warm. The doctor does not refer to relations with mothers or mistresses, but says, with some finality, *"La bonne conduite est la mère de la gayeté,"* from which one can draw one's own conclusions. Above all he recommends careful attention to the first onset of illness, and his definitive advice, with which it is hard to disagree, is this: if writing makes you ill, give it up.

So much for mid-eighteenth-century pragmatism. Yet the unbiased reader may find in Dr Tissot's list of symptoms all those to which constant reference is made in the present book. The main difference is the insistence of the nineteenth-century authors under discussion on the primacy of Art and the sacrifices which this entails. It would seem that if Art is to be preferred to Nature then the pact will be binding. *"J'ai cultivé mon hystérie avec jouissance et terreur,"* writes Baudelaire, and continues: *"Maintenant j'ai toujours le vertige, et aujourdhui, 23 janvier, 1862 j'ai subi un singulier avertissement, j'ai senti passer sur moi le vent de l'aile de l'imbécilité."* He conflates the two symptoms: the mental effort which was deliberate but in the end involuntary, and the physical disorder. It is difficult to establish which of the two produced *"le vertige"*.

What is not in any doubt is that it was the mental set that brought in its train the sexual disgust, the deliberate self-degradation, the risk of infection, the rapidity of the progress of the venereal disease, and the inevitable and terrible death. But the original imbalance produced the symptoms of a sickness which would have been entirely foreign to Dr Tissot, for it involved hatred, contempt, disgust, a freely indulged ridicule of society and *"la bonne conduite"*, an anti-democratic stance, an admiration for disorders as signs of superiority, an adoption of regimes of work that were intrinsically suicidal, an unassuageable grief, an attempt to fill one's emotional life with the promotion and prolongation of restrictive family ties, and last, but not least, a slight but damaging lack of perspective concerning one's own work. Flaubert considered *La Tentation de Saint-Antoine* a masterpiece. The brothers Goncourt, as recorded in the preface to *Chérie* of 1884, considered that they had contributed to the cultural history of the nineteenth century by reviving the art of the eighteenth century, by popularizing the art of Japan, and by inventing the working-class novel. They were wrong on all three counts.

By the same token Baudelaire, hysterical, excessive, unpleasant, and more than occasionally down at heel, was not a very good dandy.

Alphonse Daudet, patiently suffering, was not even an exceptional writer. Yet by the second half of the nineteenth century, the profession of writing had something sacerdotal about it, and men of letters were particularly assiduous in promoting the object of their cult. This may be seen as terminal Romanticism, the illness described so presciently by Zola in *L'Œuvre*, in which the painter Claude Lantier neglects his wife and child for his impossible and unrealizable masterpiece and eventually hangs himself in front of it while his child dies of neglect and his wife goes unloved.

Zola was thought by his contemporaries to be a crude fellow, without the superior sensitivity necessary for admission to the temple of Art. Yet Zola himself perceived Romanticism, which he said had obsessed him in his early years, as a form of illness in itself. Romanticism, in the popular contemporary usage of the term, is said to be incurable (as in, "He is incurably Romantic"). To Zola this was quite literally true, and he strove to set before the public of his day sturdy, middle-of-the-road, no-nonsense geniuses, a Sandoz, a Bongrand, who, in addition to their stout physical health, are endowed with normal family ties and dispositions of great generosity and sweetness. If these characters are less interesting than Madame Bovary or Renée Mauperin they are much more viable; they do not die. And it is interesting to remember that when Zola became a father, late in life, he ceased to give much care or attention to his fictional creations, which declined in power. As Baudelaire noted, *"Plus un homme cultive les arts, moins il bande,"* adding, as the dandy's corollary, *"La fouterie est le lyrisme du peuple."*

To return to Professor Williams's thesis. Its most notable characteristic is the similarity it bears to certain naturalist novels. I was impressed, when reading it, by the mastery of a certain vocabulary, the tracking down of technical terms, their presentation as the total explanation of what he himself has shown to be complex. But Professor Williams also discusses the contributory causes in a way that suggests that a whole life's decisions may be involved, that there may indeed be a wish that is ultimately responsible for such an unhappy end. Perhaps these contributory causes could have been discussed with greater sympathy. For this is painful material.

Dr Tissot could have done nothing with such patients but advise them to give up writing. It was the sad and desperate determination of Baudelaire, Jules de Goncourt, Flaubert, Maupassant and Daudet to regard the act of writing as the justification of an otherwise failed life. This it was. But they did not believe, as so many non-writers believe, that writing was a therapeutic exercise. As the subjects of the present study show, the only cure for the pains of living that writing brings about is the most final cure of all.

16

In Pursuit of Happiness *

O NE SHOULD START NEAR the end, in 1835. France's least likely
diplomat, the consul at Civitavecchia, is writing his memoirs.
Unfortunately they will only cover the first eighteen years of his life,
and for a singular reason: in remembering his first moment of happiness the writer will be so overcome that he will be unable to continue.
He will realize with a shock that he is fifty-three years old, and for an
unguarded moment he will show himself to be an ageing, even an old,
man. *"Je suis très froid aujourd'hui, le temps est gris, je souffre un peu."* His
profound discouragement, rarely in evidence, is palpable in this line.
Yet, he says, he would not hesitate to begin his life all over again. But
he could not finish the book, and thus one of the great documents in
the history of self-knowledge was aborted.

Robert Alter's excellent and balanced biography of Stendhal might
be subtitled, "As a man grows older", for he succeeds in conveying
what Stendhal himself registered with such dismay: the passage of
time. Eternally disguised, or so he hoped, as a graceful stripling,
eternally confounded by the hypocrisies of life which he had taken
such trouble to master, Stendhal found himself outwitted, at the age
of fifty, by all his dreams and stratagems. His tardy decision to marry a
woman outside the confines of his usual requirements – Giulia Rinieri
was neither emotionally extravagant nor capricious – was thwarted;

*Robert Alter, *Stendhal. A Biography*. George Allen & Unwin. *The Times Literary
Supplement*, 30 May 1980.

he was reduced to performing his consular duties in Civitavecchia; and, supreme irony, when not checking loads of grain, sugar and fabric, he sat in one of those towers which are his greatest fictional image and metaphor, alone, but not delivered from the exertions imposed by his personality, flicking pieces of paper into the sea below his window. It is how we should remember him.

For it is easy, or relatively easy, to remember Stendhal as a young man. His own account of his first eighteen years, in *La Vie de Henry Brulard*, presents more emphatically and memorably than any latter-day biographer could the facts of his early life, and ends with a moment of distress, brought on not by the painful childhood memories he has so graphically described but by the realization that he is middle-aged, stout, and more than a little weary. The conclusion of *Henry Brulard* contains all the keys to Stendhal's writing: the combination of cynicism and yearning in the recapitulation of youthful ambitions, the refusal to describe the random moment of happiness for fear of destroying it, and the strange final pages, in which he understands that at the time of writing he is no longer living on hope but on the very memory of hope.

It is the image of a life which did not quite go according to plan. On the surface witty, popular, salaried, published, even loved, Stendhal failed to close the wound dealt by those who loved him and died, or did not love him but still died. With the death of his mother, he noted, his emotional life ended (he was seven years old at the time). On hearing of the death of his adored Méthilde Dembowski, he wrote, in his occasionally effective English, "Death of my life". But it was not so, or not to the historian. By Stendhal's standards, and by virtue of one of those ironies which he so treasured, the successful part of his life was entirely posthumous. For this reason it was not enjoyed, was not dealt with to the same degree in further autobiographical writings, and was attended by clowning and boredom. Sensible plans dissolved into reasonable disappointment. Books were left unfinished. At the end he died almost anonymously, of apoplexy, in a Paris street, having given to the world of literature the unforgettable memory of Fabrice del Dongo, becalmed into sublimity, in his citadel in the forest, the Charterhouse of Parma: a formless, carelessly introduced, but utterly convincing retreat in which to end one's life. Despite its celebrated opening sentences it is the conclusion of this novel which contains its essence. Whether the publisher excised some of the last paragraph or not is hardly relevant. That all but breathless reaching of the goal, that strange rightness and finality, that sense that nothing more need be said, conform to Stendhal's own dictum, *"Dans les arts il faut toucher profondément et laisser un souvenir."*

Although Stendhal perceives himself as a failure, Fabrice, his alter ego, comes out of much the same tribulations an undoubted hero, as does Julien Sorel, although the latter's heroism is vitiated by his peasant temperament. The reasons for this dualism are interesting, and not attributable directly to the alchemy of fiction. In 1811 Stendhal wrote in his *Journal*, *"Heureux, j'aurais été charmant."* He was concerned, as usual, with the pursuit of happiness, the great unrealized goal of his life. That mythic state was compounded of Italy, and a loved woman, and a maternal smile, and an aria by Cimarosa, and the exaltation of youth, and the glow of a canvas by Correggio, all coming together and producing not merely pleasure but a transformation of the very consciousness of life itself.

There was no other world for this unbeliever: the materials given seemed to him precious enough. But his glimpses of happiness remained intermittent, and expanded only by memory and association. For this he both congratulated and blamed himself. Eternally struggling on towards the realization of the bliss he had perceived – in the sound of church bells above Rolle, at the opera in Novara, during a firework display, at the precise moment when a girl leaned her head on his shoulder in order (perhaps) to see better – he perceived with a dismay that only the greatest heroism permitted him to encompass the fact that he was not perhaps equipped to possess it. What he says is, If I had been happy I would have been charming. What he means is, If I had been charming I would have been happy.

He was an unlikely candidate for the pursuit of happiness. A narrow and confined childhood, the eternal need to earn money and position and favour, a stocky and graceless body, thin hair and bad teeth, a physical bravery that implies indifference, no home but a chosen place of exile, and a lack of true worldliness for which he strove ferociously to compensate by measuring up to the rules of the game, even when no game was being played, are not heroic traits. Henry Beyle: it is a functionary's name. It was as a functionary in the army and at the court of Napoleon that he made his not inconsiderable career until the Bourbon restoration, when even his carefully learned cynicism left him unprepared to jockey for a government position in Paris. He left for Italy once more, announcing that as he lacked further occupation he would turn to writing, much as one smoked a cigar after dinner, in order to pass the time.

It is a fine dandyish moment. Even he, who claimed to be writing for 1885 or 1935, could hardly have known then that he was about to introduce into the art of fiction a whole new technique to describe different refractions of consciousness. It is even difficult to ascertain whether he knew what he was doing for the Romantic Movement as a whole: investing it with a dimension of energy which it soon lost but which true devotees find again and again, even today, in their own experience. Yet throughout his life he used other people's works or acts to get himself going, and sometimes this shows. He began as a plagiarist, in his *Histoire de la peinture en Italie*, and his lives of Haydn, Mozart and Metastasio. He ended as the most unlikely and most unassailable of authorities on love, felicity, and the politics of aspiration.

The peculiar and rebarbative glories of Stendhal's writings are not confined to his fiction, although in the creation of his heroes, Julien Sorel, Fabrice del Dongo, Lucien Leuwen, and, one might add, the unladylike Lamiel, he gives us the transformed self to which he directed all his efforts and which was closely bound up with physical appearance and demeanour: youthful, graceful, loved by women, able to disarm the criticism of men, endowed with heroic powers of choice, favoured at the end with an exaltation which others might call grace. Julien's musings in his prison cell, when for the first and last time in his life he is delivered from calculation and secrecy and ambition and hypocrisy, have a curiously becalmed quality absent from many a more orthodox deathbed. Mme de Rênal comes and goes, without a thought for the injuries he has done her, and they have perhaps become mother and child, impervious in their symbiosis to danger from outside. Entranced, Julien begs to be allowed to keep his ideal life, rather than manoeuvre for the continuation of his real life on earth. He dies well. Similarly Fabrice, to all intents and purposes, dies in his citadel at the moment when he withdraws from the world.

The great and brave woman who loves him, La Sanseverina, left behind without him, also dies well. *"La comtesse en un mot réunissait toutes les apparences du bonheur, mais elle ne survécut que fort peu de temps à Fabrice, qu'elle adorait, et qui ne passa qu'une année dans sa Chartreuse."* There is no happy end for Lucien Leuwen or for Lamiel, for Stendhal clearly did not know what to do with them. They were both condemned to live, in married felicity in the one instance, coldly and with malice aforethought in the other, and of both of these conditions Stendhal had not the slightest experience. He gives us four great exemplars of the heroic way of life, Julien and Mme de Rênal, Fabrice and Sanseverina, and he proves that there can be great nobility in the true perception of one's own character, or what other Romantic writers would have called soul.

For Stendhal is a Romantic with a difference. Not only does he eschew the grand gesture – Berlioz conducting with a drawn sword, Victor Hugo on his rock – he views any sort of grand gesture with undiminished eighteenth-century scepticism. There is no hypocrisy in mathematics, he says, to explain his first choice of career. How much rich material, therefore, he must have found in those years between the Restoration and the Revolution of 1848, which he did not live to see. For the specialist in hypocrisy hunted down precisely those scenes from a Paris salon, those chronicles of 1830, as he subtitled *Armance* and *Le Rouge et le noir*, to nourish his zest for the futile, the presumptuous, the nefarious. He brings no indignation to bear against these qualities, merely his own fine sense of ridicule, polished to perfection by many years of being employed against himself.

Yet he participates in the Romantic adventure. It may be that those who see Romanticism as a synonym for inertia, passivity, exclusion, will be unwilling to find an ally in Stendhal, who celebrates it as a continuation of Napoleonic conquest. He was not alone in perceiving this possibility. Balzac, to cite only the most obvious name, stated explicitly that what Napoleon had started with the sword he would finish with the pen, and produced six novels a year to prove it. Our fathers made war, says Stendhal more obliquely; we make love. This is a witty encapsulation of the new predicament. With the Empire won and lost, with society, religion, even the days of the week so recently banished and restored, with Napoleon dying in exile, and a king even less remarkable than his predecessor once more on the throne of France, there was not only trauma but a necessary displacement of human activity. Those who had seen and admired Napoleon – and Stendhal had done both, conversing with him outside the gates of Moscow – retained both a belief in superhuman power and a glorification of impulse. An ideal of effortlessness, of the sure-footedness that characterized Napoleon at his most successful, remained with them for life, as did an ideal of Napoleonic rapidity: Constant wrote *Adolphe* in fifteen days, Hugo wrote *Hernani* in a month, Stendhal wrote *La Chartreuse de Parme* in fifty-two days and made only notional revisions. If Stendhal joins up at all with the more standard Romantic artists it is because he shares with them the fantasy of the supreme emotional adventure. If he surpasses them it is because he knows how to convince us, by extraordinary means, that this is actually taking place.

For Stendhal's reticence is as surprising as his energy. In this most confessional of literary epochs, when most writers decided to forgo their traditional sense of honour, Stendhal retains his, and turns it to wry account. His inability to finish *La Vie de Henry Brulard*, because he has come to a moment of analloyed personal happiness which he fears to spoil by what must inevitably seem to him a tedious description, was scrutinized for what it involved. After all, that moment of happiness amounted to nothing more than a ride on horseback along the shores of Lake Geneva, hearing the church bells ring in a nearby town. There would have been no indiscretion in describing it. Yet Stendhal is right in thinking that more words would not have enhanced the experience, might indeed have muddied its essence. The thing signified, glanced at, alluded to, remembered, became all the more powerful for not being shared.

And for this reason Stendhal was able to bring about two of the most famous scenes in the history of the French novel, famous because they are not there, and because, in withholding them, the author creates a powerful sense of what is hidden between two people who make love. Julien Sorel, fresh from the sawmill, his jacket under his arm, arrives tearfully at the house of Monsieur de Rênal, where he is to be tutor to the children. He is little more than a child himself, but he knows Latin, admires Napoleon, and is very ambitious. He conceives it his Napoleonic duty to seduce the innocent and virtuous Madame de Rênal, and various heavily plotted moves are made in this direction. She, poor lady, falls in love with him, and he, although he does not yet know it, with her. Honour demands that he visit her in her bedroom and make her his "conquest" (the very word is Napoleonic).

The scene is obviously crucial, for the rest of the novel turns on it: Julien's removal to a seminary in Besançon, his employment in Paris, his decision to marry the daughter of a nobleman, Madam de Rênal's revenge, his shot at her, his imprisonment and death. Yet we are told nothing about it. Or rather what we are told removes it from our experience and confines it to the secret realms in which these matters take place. Of the night spent in Madame de Rênal's bedroom, Stendhal merely remarks, *"Quelques heures après, quand Julien sortit de la chambre de madame de Rênal, on eut pu dire, en style de roman, qu'il n'avait plus rien à désirer."* And later, after the even more intoxicating seduction of Mathilde de la Mole, we read, *"La vertu de Julien fut égale à son bonheur . . ."* Even the use of the word *"vertu"*, here used to indicate prowess, removes the matter from our vulgar scrutiny. Those occasions for rapturous explicitness, those very scenes which now sell romantic novels, in the debased sense of the term, are omitted. Loftily, Stendhal implies that they are none of our business. Nor are they his. For he was Henry Beyle, not Julien Sorel, and he would not commit the double indiscretion of dealing explicitly with an imagined or treasured experience. As he says in another context, *"La passion a sa pudeur."*

He had both, and the combination is very potent. He also had the energy to contend with the passion and the delicacy to preserve the necessary reticence. For this reason one assesses the corpulent salon wit, with his sometimes embarrassing behaviour, as one of the Happy Few. Perhaps that ride along the shores of Lake Geneva was the keenest sensation he ever knew. Perhaps a less honourable and emotional man would have perceived in Méthilde Dembowski ("Death of my life") a rather inappropriate agency for annihilating despair. Perhaps those elegant calculations that he would be read in 1885 or 1935 proceed from extreme discouragement. He was too circumspect, or too brave, to let us know. For he trusted that hints would be picked up by members of that band of initiates, the Happy Few, to whom he dedicated *La Chartreuse de Parme.*

The dedication, significantly, comes at the end; it is the afterword.

Just who these people are has never been properly established. Stendhal, in his roundabout way, would claim an eighteenth-century source, the second chapter of Goldsmith's *Vicar of Wakefield*. Others might think of Shakespeare and *Henry V*. The true meaning would seem to lie half-way between kindred spirits and *"âmes d'élite"*, and the qualification for membership six months of unrequited love and the ability to deal with it in the manner demonstrated in *De l'Amour*. Many readers of Stendhal confess themselves to be outside the charmed circle. Fortunately those who feel called to examine such a life are already inside it. The biographer, whose humble task it is to investigate these matters, will experience in return some of the tonic effects of his subject's personality. Robert Alter passes the test very well indeed.

17

Corinne and Her *Coups de Foudre* *

DON PEDRO DE SOUZA e Hostein, Duke of Parmella, has earned his place in history less as Prime Minister of Portugal than as one of Mme de Staël's lovers and as the model for the hero of her novel *Corinne*. Their affair lasted a bare two months, which was appropriate: she was thirty-nine, stout, florid and vehement, while he was twenty-four, handsome, well-bred and disenchanted. What drew them together is anybody's guess. What drove them apart was no doubt her unsuitability (although she was the most famous woman in Europe and the only enemy whose influence Napoleon feared) and her usual *modus operandi* in affairs of the heart: convulsions, long accusing letters, expertly induced guilt, announcements that she was dying or would soon take her life, and occasional attempts at kidnap, using as intermediary one of her children or friends or lovers or hangers-on: Schlegal, Sismondi, Mme Récamier, or the beleaguered Benjamin Constant.

It is important to realize that Mme de Staël was not promiscuous. Although, by my count, Souza was her ninth *coup de foudre*, none, except the wretched Constant, who, like her father, called her Minette, ever gave her what she craved: this might be described as fidelity with enthusiasm, the love she originally received from her father Necker, France's Minister of Finance, who praised, encouraged, marvelled,

*Madame de Staël, Don Pedro de Souza: Correspondence. Edited by Beatrix d'Andlau. Gallimard. The Times Literary Supplement, 14 March 1980.

refrained from criticism, and admired. That he had time to be anything but a father to his daughter is altogether surprising. Presumably financial affairs seemed to him a simple matter in comparison. That Mme de Staël found time to be anything but a daughter to such a father, whom she worshipped, and whose every memorandum she edited and published, is also a matter of some remark.

It was perhaps after his death in 1804, when Mme de Staël was dancing at a ball in Berlin, that her emotional health began to suffer. Although her activities and her extravagances continued unabated, there is something profoundly disturbing about her continued demands for love, or, even after she had been resoundingly abandoned or repudiated, for friendship. She never changed. Souza was succeeded by Prosper de Barante (also twenty four), and by the young Graf Moritz O'Donnell, the Viennese Irishman who wrote her a letter saying that his honour would not permit him to go on loving her. By cunning and determination, both of a fairly infantile variety, she kept up a thread of acquaintance, if only by invitations to Coppet (irresistible) or by letters of breathtaking unfairness to which the victims found themselves forced to reply. What she could not do was let go, which would mean doing without love. She is perhaps history's most oustanding case of *Torschlusspanik*: the panic at the shutting of the door.

Although this is a serious matter it looks ridiculous. It was this extraordinary woman's fate to be a laughing-stock. In Paris, in Berlin, in Vienna, in Stockholm, in London, ladies and gentlemen of fashion saw only her hefty arms and bosom, too generously displayed, her elaborate turbans and shawls, her ever-open mouth, and the spill of paper she rolled and unrolled compulsively between her fingers. This same audience may have read her novel *Delphine*, in which the author states, *"Il ne faut à une femme, pour être heureuse, que la certitude d'être parfaitement aimée,"* would certainly have read her confessional *Corinne*, would have heard of the publicity surrounding

De la littérature, but could not have read *De l'Allemagne*, which Napoleon suppressed, or the *Dix années d'exil* to which he subjected her, or the magnificent *Considérations sur les principaux évènements de la révolution française*.

While her importance was acknowledged soon after her death in 1817 – a complete edition of her collected works appeared in 1820 – she was always good for a laugh while she was alive. For had she not, at the age of forty-five, allowed herself to be loved by a young man of twenty-three, as stupid as he was handsome? And had she not, with great difficulty, given birth to his son, who turned out to be retarded? And did she not return in triumph to the Paris which Napoleon had forbidden her, only to suffer a stroke while ascending a staircase to one of those diplomatic receptions which would have been incomplete without her? She died, aged fifty-one, perhaps of an overdose of opium, nursed by her young latter-day husband, John Rocca, who did not survive her six months.

She was the centre of all lives, except perhaps her own, for that vacancy could only be filled by the object of her love, whoever he might be at the time. Unfortunately her demands were rather exacting: the lover had to be handsome, young, aristocratic, brilliant, and worldly. Schlegel and Sismondi were barred, although never dispensed with, because although faithful unto death they lacked too many of these characteristics. But into the charmed category came Narbonne and Montmorency and François de Pange and Ribbing and Souza, and perhaps an Irishman named O'Brien, and Barante and O'Donnell. The two men who matched her intellectually, Talleyrand and Constant, tried to get away. Only Talleyrand managed it. Only Talleyrand could. Constant, after years of inharmonious intimacy, read her his novel, *Adolphe*, reduced her to hysterics, fell in love with her friend, Mme Récamier, and ended up by going home to his wife. In comparison Don Pedro only qualifies for an idyll. On the Richter scale of Mme de Staël's emotional fortunes Don Pedro averages about three out of ten. He was handsome, young, brilliant etc.; he did not last. He returned once or twice, and shortly after their last meeting he married a girl of sixteen.

In December 1804 Mme de Staël obtained permission to travel to Italy; no doubt Napoleon wished to enjoy his coronation celebrations without the benefit of her comments. She arrived in Rome in February 1805, accompanied by her three children and their tutor, August Wilhelm Schlegel. The purpose of her visit was to write a book about Italy, though she had never been there before. She was greeted, as usual, with great enthusiasm, and a singular honour was paid her by the Arcadian Academy, which named her "pastourelle", that is to say a pastoral or lyrical singer. Present at this interesting ceremony was Don Pedro de Souza, blue-eyed, black-haired, suffering from Romantic melancholy, and filling in as *chargé d'affaires* until the new Portuguese minister arrived in Rome. Mme de Staël could not ignore so obvious a portent.

For two months, with a break for a journey to Naples, she lived her Roman idyll, the high point of which appears to have been a visit to the Colosseum by moonlight. She kept her head, however, and until 14 May the tone of her letters is genial, warm, excited, but in no sense threatening. She must indeed have been a delightful friend at this point, although Don Pedro, with rather unflattering caution, emphasizes his respect for her. It was when she took to writing poetry to him that matters began to lose their social gloss, and when she left Rome for Florence at the beginning of May she appears to have suffered an access of amorous despair, of the kind which characterizes most of her dealings with the rest of the world.

From Florence she wrote him the letter that has survived their friendship and is known to most *Staëliens*:

> *Rome et vous sont inséparables dans ma mémoire, je*
> *n'ai compris que par vous les délices de ce séjour; mon*

*imagination n'avait point encore peuplé le désert, je vous ai
aimé et tout s'est animé pour moi, les beaux-arts, la nature,
et jusqu'aux souvenirs du passé qui me faisaient mal et
dont j'ai appris à jouir. Deux mois de ma vie sont votre
œuvre, ne seriez-vous tenté de me faire don encore de
quelques mois ensemble?*

She realized that there might be no return of her love *"car la destinée
ne nous a pas fait contemporains"*. However, a way could be found out
of this difficulty if Don Pedro would marry her daughter Albertine.
The fact that the child was only eight years old at the time merely
encouraged Mme de Staël to think in terms of a long engagement.

On 15 May she wrote, *"vous revoir à Rome et mourir là près de vous"*.
Souza replied scrupulously that he missed the intellectual stimulus of
her company: she was his *"céleste amie"*, his *"divine amie"*. But Mme de
Staël, who had the courage of the true Romantic when it came to
taking risks, overlooked his prudence and invited him to Coppet,
urging him to break all previous engagements. *"Cher Don Pèdre,
n'appelez pas déraison ce qui est inspiré par l'élan de l'âme, c'est la véritable
raison, celle des hommes supérieurs, des coeurs passionnés qui seuls ont senti
la vie, qui seuls auront puisé dans la coupe céleste."* She would wait for him
at Coppet until October.

In the meantime she was proceeding home by way of Bologna,
Venice, Milan, Turin. She reached Switzerland at the end of June, and
there found distraction in the shape of the young Prosper de Barante,
son of the Prefect of Geneva, also to be pressed into service when
Corinne was under way. Barante occurred at the right moment, for by
September Souza had engaged himself to a Mlle de Perron. Mme de
Staël still waited for news of his arrival at Coppet. She waited until the
end of December, and the letter that finally came brought her news of
the forthcoming marriage. Souza makes little of the matter, and goes
on to speak of mutual friends; he is skilful, delicate, and only a trifle

embarrassed. With great panache Mme de Staël wrote back and congratulated him. This had the desired efect, and in February 1806 Souza arrived at Coppet.

Naturally Mme de Staël wanted to take him to Paris, but Napoleon's decrees had forbidden her to approach within forty leagues of the capital. For some reason she went to Auxerre, where she reported herself to be dying of boredom, while Souza went to Paris. She then rented the nearby château of Vincelles; she also tried to maintain contact with Don Pedro by commissioning him to translate the *Lusiads* into French, a task which he soon abandoned. A letter from Dijon makes frenzied plans for a last meeting in Auxerre, but she was restless, and her movements were unpredictable. She met Souza for the last time on 15 or 16 September at Argeville, Constant's farm near Paris. She wept as she heard his horse galloping away. *"Je ne sais que cela, je ne sais que cela . . . Adieu, cher, cher Dom Pèdre, oh! quand dirai-je ce nom avec un avenir?"*

She was never able to do this. He wrote her a few more letters, mainly rather dull. He broke off his engagement to Mlle de Perron, did enormously well in the army and the diplomatic corps, married the sixteen-year-old Eugenia Telles de Gama, became Minister in Spain, and finally Prime Minister of Portugal. Mme de Staël published *Corinne* in 1897, saw the type of *De l'Allemagne* broken up on Napoleon's orders, went to Russia, just ahead of the French army, on to Sweden, where she favoured Bernadotte's cause, and finally, before her triumphant but too long delayed return to Paris, to England. There she attended a party given by Lord Lansdowne at Bowood, where she glimpsed Don Pedro among the guests. He was thirty-five and still handsome; she was nearly fifty and sadly altered. It was their last meeting, and it was an accident. There are no more letters.

Yet literature has a way of taking care of these matters. The Don Pedro we know is Oswald, Lord Nelvil, the improbably named hero of

Corinne. A divine melancholy emanates from Oswald, and the doctors, fearing for his health, have sent him to Italy. In fact he is incurable, for he suffers from guilt at not having complied with his father's wishes, and it is the death of his father which has brought about the alteration in his health. Although his heart is in disorder, Oswald's perfect manners keep this fact concealed. He is the soul of honour and goodness; after the sea passage rough sailors flock to him, and chorus, *"Mon cher seigneur, puissiez-vous être heureux!"* He awakes in Rome to the sound of cannon fire, and is told that this announces the crowning on the Capitol of Corinne, poet, writer, improviser, and *"une des plus belles personnes de Rome"*. She is twenty-six years old. The streets are decorated; crowds gather. *"Vive Corinne!"* they shout, *"vive le génie, vive la beauté"*. Enter Corinne, wearing a white dress and a shawl wound round her black curls. Her modesty and her noble bearing bring tears to Oswald's eyes. A eulogy is read, extolling her gaiety, grace and eloquence. Oswald is particularly struck by the concluding words:

> *Oui, voyez Corinne, si cette double existence qu'elle vous donnera peut vous être longtemps assurée; mais ne la voyez pas, si vous êtes condamné à la quitter; vous chercheriez en vain, tant que vous vivrez, cette âme créatrice qui partageait et multipliait vos sentiments et vos pensées, vous ne la retrouverez jamais.*

It is all there: Mme de Staël's dreams of youth and beauty, of acknowledgement of her uniqueness, and the completely historical detail of her meeting with Souza during the ceremony at the Arcadian Academy. More dreams and wishes follow. Oswald will not see anyone but Corinne, who is fascinated by his mystery and reticence. She writes him a letter which sets the seal on their intimacy, and they leave together to visit Rome. There follows the long traveller's guide which Mme de Staël presumably had in mind when she first set out for Italy, for the full title of the novel is *Corinne, ou l'Italie*. Further observations on Italian art, music, drama, and the Italian character follow. By this time Oswald wonders whether he should ask Corinne to marry him, but is put off by her foreign ways, and by his dying father's wish that he should marry Lucile Edgermond, a suitable young English person.

It is by now clear that Corinne too has a guilty secret, but she postpones her explanation until she and Oswald have enjoyed a visit to Naples. (Mme de Staël in fact went to Naples without Don Pedro.) Corinne, after a more than usually sumptuous performance, accompanied on the lyre, confesses that she is the half-sister of Lucile Edgermond. Oswald's father had thought of making a match between Corinne and his son, but had found Corinne too excitable, and settled for the younger girl. Oswald returns to England. There he finds Lucile. She is modest, pure, and suitable. She is also sixteen years old.

From this point on the novel changes from an idyll to a tragedy, its personal meaning for Mme de Staël conveyed by the beauty of the writing. Corinne, consumed with anxiety, waits for letters from Oswald:

> . . . elle n'avait d'autre évènement, d'autre variété dans la vie que les lettres d'Oswald, et l'irrégularité de la poste, pendant l'hiver, excitait chaque jour en elle le tourment de l'attente, et souvent cette attente était trompée. Elle se promenait tous les matins sur le bord du canal, dont les eaux sont assoupies sous le poids des larges feuilles appelées les lis des eaux. Elle attendait la gondole noire qui apportait les lettres de Venise; elle était parvenue à la distinguer à une très grande distance, et le coeur lui battait avec une affreuse violence dès qu'elle l'apercevait: le messager descendait de la gondole, quelquefois il disait, Madame, il n'y a point de lettres, et continuait ensuite paisiblement le reste de ses affaires, comme si rien n'était si simple que de n'avoir point de lettres.

Finally, her looks gone, her health in decline, Corinne decides to follow Oswald to Scotland. She arrives to find a ball in progress to celebrate his engagement to Lucile, and watches from the dark garden as he appears on a balcony, with the lights of the ballroom behind him: the brilliant original scene from which many later Gothic romances derive. Waylaying a peasant, Corinne gives him her ring and a letter containing the words, *"Vous êtes libre."* She falls into a swoon, is ill, goes home to Italy, and dies. Mme de Staël's unpurged childishness has her die in the presence of Oswald and his wife. Both are heartbroken. Italy mourns.

Mme de Staël was fond of enacting the climactic tirades of Racine's heroines on the stage at Coppet, and perhaps she was the only living person to embody female passion as Racine describes it. That so great a Romantic should be such an onerous lover is a paradox appropriate to the age, or indeed to any age. She was too clever to remain in ignorance of this. In the latter part of *Corinne* the bitter regrets – for lack of youth, health, beauty – are all the more memorable for being so innocently stated. Mme de Staël, waiting for letters, and realizing that they would not arrive, was also too clever not to notice that she inspired discomfort and finally fear in her lovers.

The Romantic hero is rarely a match for the Romantic heroine, as Don Pedro and his successors were to discover, and Mme de Staël came to regard male caution with contempt: *"Les âmes passionnées se trahissent de mille manières, et ce que l'on contient toujours est bien faible."* It is only fitting that she should have the last word, for that is frequently all she got.

Many more of these letters must await publication. Mme Beatrix d'Andlau, who has already edited the letters of Mme de Staël to Narbonne and Ribbing, sets a high standard, all the more effective for being so self-effacing.

18

A Nun of Art*

JUDITH GAUTIER WAS exceedingly famous in her own day and is completely forgotten in ours. She would have been famous had she not written a line for being the daughter of Théophile, the *poète impeccable* with his Merovingian hairstyle and conquistador's garments. She would have been famous as the offspring of a liaison irregular even by modern standards, for her mother, Ernesta Grisi, was Gautier's second choice of partner, since he remained enamoured of Ernesta's sister Carlotta, with whom he often sought refuge: he married neither of them. Judith would have been more justifiably famous as a great beauty: countless admirers, and even the brothers Goncourt, were to speak of her black eyes, her matte white skin and her Hindu profile. She might even have been famous as one of Victor Hugo's last passions; she would certainly have been famous for her Platonic association with Wagner. But she was most famous of all for her stories, fables of the mythic East, which she wrote with disconcerting fluency and unabashed idealism throughout her life, although she never set foot outside Europe, and indeed hardly travelled at all except for visits to Brussels and various German towns, and of course to Tribschen and to Wahnfried, to visit Wagner and attend the first nights of his operas.

What made her Orientalism so strange – and on the strength of her

---

*Joanna Richardson, *Judith Gautier: A Biography*. Quartet. *The Times Literary Supplement*, 6 March 1987.

stories it is hardly believable – was that she was a scholar: she spoke and wrote Chinese, surrounded herself with Chinese and Japanese artefacts, and was convinced, on the grounds of affinity alone, that she had been born in the wrong country. In later life she wore kimonos, corresponded with the Emperor of Annam, and kept a menagerie of snakes, lizards, cats and tortoises in her red lacquer apartment in the rue Washington. She would have been singular even if she had not been famous, but she was also widely read in her own lifetime, and as the Hindu profile survived the ravages of age, and as she was well-meaning if indolent, many young men flocked to her door and news of her continued to circulate. She became the first woman member of the jury of the Académie Goncourt, and continued to write, though not to bestir herself as she had once done, until her death in 1900 in the small villa she had had built in Brittany, near Dinard. Her companion at the end was not one of her previously ardent admirers, all of whom had predeceased her, but a gauche young woman of Alsatian background, Suzanne Meyer-Zundel. The two women wrote poetry to each other and were eventually buried in the same grave.

As is the case with most famous beauties of the nineteenth century, it is extremely hard to discern the lineaments of desire in the corpulent bodies and heavy jowled faces that survive in the photographs of the time. Abundant oiled hair, busts hoisted to collar-bone level, confident jawlines and bulldog necks belie the head rested poetically on the hand or the gaze inclined on the middle distance. Gautier, dressed as a gipsy king, perhaps in an effort to disguise his incessant labour as a journalist, looks grimy and theatrical. Hugo, bristling white beard climbing to meet his bristling white hair, might be a sea captain (the comparison was made in his lifetime) or the retired inventor of an improved kind of sulphur match, rather than the authentic spirit of Romantic passion in love and politics. Catulle Mendès, Judith's disappointing husband, was famed in his day for his seductiveness, his hint of corruption, his *ange déchu* beauty; in the Fernand Desmoulin

engraving which Joanna Richardson reproduces, he looks startled and
finicky. Only Wagner stands up to physical scrutiny, largely, one
suspects, because he remained thin. Judith herself rapidly became
mountainous, and was more or less obliged to wear flowing Oriental
garments. Sargent painted her standing beside her piano, in a cream
taffeta peignoir; it is possible to see in the slightly thickened features
and the noble decorated coiffure the Japanese and therefore highly
fashionable charm of this woman who exerted such a spell over men
of letters, young and old, whatever her own private inclination might
have been, and who survived her early fame with her reputation
for goodness intact and even enhanced by her lazy and impassive
hospitality, or perhaps simply by the fact that she could, in the end, be
compared with no one but her own illustrious father. For she was
Gautier's daughter to the last, despite her Oriental imaginings, and she
earns her place in literature as a late Parnassian, a fervent publicizer
and celebrator of the Japanese taste, a forerunner of Pierre Loti and
Pierre Louys, both of whom she knew when they were young and she
was old, and possibly the highest incantation of that languishing
sexless ardour that can also be discerned in Huysmans and Gustave
Moreau, and which may be the true decadence.

Yet she herself remained an innocent, at least on paper. When she
converted, at the end of her life, into an animal-loving solitary who
had renounced human passion, she may not have been entirely honest
with her public; there is little evidence to suggest that she had ever
valued the love of men or that she had even judged it correctly.
Her marriage to Catulle Mendès filled her with disgust, not without
justification, for he was famously dissolute, and managed to father
five children by another bulldog-jawed beauty, Augusta Holmès, three
of them while he was still married. Judith Gautier may or may not
have responded to Victor Hugo, who, at the age of seventy, was still on
manoeuvres: their common language is so inflated that it is difficult to
tell exactly what is happening. This mystical language is even rather

worrying, for it oversteps the bounds of taste at every turn, and it seems that in her innocence Judith was the worst offender. She wrote to Wagner, after meeting him at Tribschen for the first time, "It is only now that I understand the felicity of Paradise, which is so extolled by the faithful: the joy of seeing God face to face." A young man seen bathing at Fécamp was compared with the Archangel Michael and so addressed in a poem which she wrote to celebrate his beauty, while Mme Meyer-Zundel is likened to the Virgin Mary on the strength of having sent a liver pâté to the rue Washington.

And yet this prose is not negligible. Perhaps it should be anthologized, rather than allowed to remain embedded in fantasy, although it is the strength of the informing fantasy that gives it its power. An example, from a story called *Le Prince à la tête sanglante*, will convey the peculiar resonance of her style, and possibly its addictive qualities:

> *De l'autre côté de l'étang un frangipanier, merveilleuse-ment, s'épanouit: aux branches nues, rien que des fleurs, de petites fleurs jaunes et blanches d'un adorable parfum; mais tout un peuple d'abeilles, d'insectes et de papillons tourbil-lonnent dans les branches fleuries, avec quel tumulte et quelle joie! Ils se gorgent, se saoulent, s'affolent; les ailes vibrent ou palpitent; des gouttes d'or, des émeraudes, des flammes, passionnément, fondent sur les pétales embaumés, les baisent, les mordent, sucent la salive mielleuse, pétris-sent la pulpe tendre gonflée d'un lait amer: par moments l'arbre semble se secouer, rejeter ces amantes insatiables; mais elles se ruent de nouveau, toujours avides, avec un frémissement plus sonore.*

This is not merely an adequate imitation of bees sipping nectar. These are heavenly bees and heavenly flowers, seen nowhere, heard nowhere on earth, certainly not in Paris, but imagined from a Chinese scroll painting, improved, made precious, succulent, amorous, yet distant, a phantom exchange between lovers and the beloved. It is Gautier's *transposition d'art* wrought up to correspond with a female fantasy, a female sensibility, and set down uncompromisingly by one who preferred her passions to be literary and cerebral, worshipful and ethereal, and who maintained her extraordinary and authentic gift amid a whirl of daily journalism, debts, and marital anxieties while continuing firmly to believe that she was spiritually Chinese or at least Oriental, a belief that enabled her to write a guide to Tokyo without ever leaving Paris. Her contemporaries were perhaps correct to hold her in awe.

She was her father's daughter in more ways than one. She was his indulged favourite and was allowed to do much as she wanted. She was, for instance, given a Chinese tutor, Tin-Tun-Ling, who is probably to be credited with imparting to her her lifelong adoration of things Chinese. She was also a working journalist, much as her father had been, and as early as 1864 made her début by reviewing the exhibition held by the Société Nationale des Beaux-Arts in *L'Artiste*, under the pseudonym Judith Walter. She was even the same kind of critic as her father, preferring to describe rather than to analyse. She wrote for all the major newspapers. She published four articles on the Chinese, Japanese and Siamese contributions to the Exposition Universelle of 1867 in *Le Moniteur*, and three articles on "Richard Wagner et la Critique" in *La Presse* in 1868. These she sent to Wagner, thus beginning a curious, fervent, and not altogether attractive enchantment which bound them together in mutual admiration. Wagner's love was of an intense and possibly insane variety, Judith's no less. When Wagner grasped her arm in 1876, she noted, "For me it was as if Christ had suddenly begun to pay court to Mary Magdalen." He perfumed his letters to her with essence of roses. She was instrumental, with her husband, Catulle Mendès, in popularizing Wagner's works in France, or rather in Paris, and whereas Baudelaire had only had the overture to *Tannhäuser* to inflame his admiration, Mendès and his wife pursued the Master's offerings at every first performance, travelling to Brussels for *Lohengrin* and to Munich for *Die Walküre*, and never ceasing in their efforts to keep these works in the forefront of the news in Paris.

What breathes through Judith Gautier's work is a sensual chastity or a chaste sensuality, all the more powerful for its being removed in time and distance from the mundane circumstances of ordinary feelings. And it is extraordinarily powerful. The childlike simplicity of the stories is interspersed with descriptions of exalted physicality, like the example quoted above. But in these stories love and death go hand in hand, and consummation is not of this world. Her own consummation is a matter of more than local interest. After a short marriage, a possible liaison with Hugo, a Platonic rapture shared with Wagner, and the admiration of many younger men, she found peace at last with a jolly girl from Mulhouse some thirty years her junior. Suzanne Mayer-Zundel possessed an unusual and indeed unchallenged gift: she was able to fashion lifelike flowers out of breadcrumbs, an endowment which earned her the nickname of Mademoiselle Mie-de-Pain. She was also rich and of a devoted disposition. Her account of their friendship, *Quinze ans auprès de Judith Gautier*, supplements Judith's autobiography, *Le Collier des Jours*, from which most of the matter of this excellent biography is taken. How far things went with Miss Breadcrumbs cannot of course be known; when they met, the twenty-two-year-old girl was clumsy and passionate and clearly unfitted for normal life as a woman, but Judith's amorous poems to her may have been part of her general withdrawal from the world of men and into the world of animals, pets and acolytes. There was, in any event, no scandal surrounding the liaison; indeed Judith Gautier's outstanding gift was her ability to impress herself on public opinion without making the slightest concession in its direction.

It is entirely fitting that towards the end of her life she became monosyllabic, and when forced to speak would use words carelessly, as if they scarcely interested her. At the same time anything written – letters, poems, the occasional article – remained wonderfully clear. She was a genuine eccentric, "a nun of art", finally at home in the rue Washington with her animals, entertaining the Emperor of Annam, dressed like a fortune-teller, feeding her guests on pineapples and loucoum and black olives, and quite firm in the belief that she was the reincarnation of a Chinese princess. Joanna Richardson does full justice to a woman who at first sight might not have much claim on the attention. It is to Miss Richardson's credit that one closes her book with a feeling of respect for this unlikely academician, whose independent life entitles her to an honourable place in the pantheon of French women of letters, from George Sand or even Mme de Staël to Colette.

19

On High Heels up Vesuvius*

IN OCTOBER 1879 FLAUBERT, then aged fifty-seven, invited Maupassant to dinner, informing him that there was a purpose behind this invitation. He wanted to burn some letters, and he did not want to do so alone. After a particularly good meal, Flaubert brought a heavy suitcase into his study and began to throw packets of letters into the fire, occasionally reading passages from them in his booming voice. This process went on until 4 a.m., not an unusual hour for Flaubert. (History does not relate whether Maupassant was equally alert.) One particularly thick bundle of letters contained a small package tied with a ribbon. This was seen to consist of a silk shoe, a rose, and a woman's handkerchief, which Flaubert kissed before he threw it into the fire. It has always been assumed, and it is assumed by the author of this book, that these relics, notably the letters, were evidence of his attachment to Louise Colet, his mistress in the late 1840s and early to mid 1850s. His letters to her, now in the Bibliothèque Municipale of Avignon, contain reports on the work in progress, which was to become *Madame Bovary*, together with remarks and maxims which form the essence of his artistic credo.

An irreverent question now arises: what happened to the other shoe? That there were two is attested by Flaubert's frequent references to them in his letters to Colet. Sartre, for whom literally nothing was

*Francine du Plessix Gray, *Rage and Fire: A Life of Louise Colet – Pioneer Feminist, Literary Star, Flaubert's Muse.* Hamish Hamilton. *The London Review of Books*, 21 July 1994.

sacred, observed that this was proof of Flaubert's fetishism, that he was satisfied to keep the woman herself at a comfortable distance and the token slippers close at hand. Remember that he was unable to visit her very often, certainly not as often as she expected him to, while he undoubtedly considered her to be a threat to his work. He needed the quiet of Croisset and the company of his mother, a virtuoso of hypochondria, rather more than that of the tempestuous Colet, whose beauty, by that stage at its peak, failed to compensate for what he rightly considered her meretricious talent as a poet. "You write verses the way a hen lays eggs," he told her.

Second question: why did Flaubert need Maupassant as a witness on this most private occasion? We know that Flaubert had a more intimate relationship with his male friends than with all women except George Sand, whom he treated with rare respect. This gives further credence to Sartre's observation that there was a homoerotic edge to Flaubert's friendships, although this was true of most of the men in the Goncourt circle, all of whom were given to sharing details of their sexual prowess. Whereas most men delight in an ardent mistress, Flaubert only desired to be ardent himself on the relatively rare occasions permitted by his particular sexual economy. An enthusiastic frequenter of brothels, an equally enthusiastic frequenter of those friends who shared his tastes, Flaubert, though not a true ascetic, held firmly to the opinion that ejaculation subverted creative energy. More to the point, he knew that the rage he experienced when Colet levelled her reproaches at him might bring on an epileptic fit, and on one occasion it did so. She looked after him skilfully, wiped his face, and afterwards assured him that he had not foamed at the mouth, although he had. Small wonder that Flaubert's genius confined him to what Henry James called the madness of art, since that is exclusive, self-inflicted, entirely wilful, and implicit with the grandiosity of the child laying claim to his domain.

Francine du Plessix Gray, in this wildly partisan and thoroughly enjoyable biography of Colet, whom she attempts to reinstate as a feminist icon and "yet another woman whose memory has been erased by the caprices of men", makes many claims for her subject, who, it has to be said, is only remembered owing to the caprice of one man, Gustave Flaubert. At the end of their affair he wrote her a spectacularly cruel letter, informing her that he no longer wished to see her. The fact that this letter survives may shed some light on Colet's masochism, although the picture that emerges from this enthusiastic account is of a determined but pathetic character who did her best, against considerable odds, to emulate more forceful women, both real and fictitious, who had achieved notoriety and acclaim on strength of character alone. These women were fatally near at hand as role models: Charlotte Corday, Mme de Staël, George Sand, and surely Corinne, Mme de Staël's eponymous heroine, beauteous, beloved, and a poetess of the highest rank. Louise Colet too wrote poetry, but we can perhaps judge its quality from the fact that her unblushing biographer refuses to include it in other than a rather lame English translation, on the grounds that "it is not a striking exemplar of French Romantic verse". From the translations it appears that the poems are abysmal. Some later poems are given in the original French. Unfortunately they are no good either.

Nevertheless we are dealing with a woman who had a life both before and after Flaubert, and whose evolution can certainly be seen as a useful example of Romantic endeavour, and a confused attempt to claim a destiny which would earn for her the type of glory she craved, and in part achieved. It is a peculiar irony that she achieved this in every area except that of her writing. We remember her as Flaubert's lover, and we remember her through his letters to her, not hers to him. And Flaubert's letters to Colet are chiefly memorable as a commentary on the work in progress, and which she obviously dealt with cleverly, as they kept on coming. It takes a particular skill to accommodate statements of the kind which have become famous, such as the claim that the artist should be immanent but invisible, like God in the universe, or the assertion, surely bewildering to one of Colet's intelligence, that her lover desired to eliminate from his work not only himself but the subject as well, so that the resulting book would be held together by the internal strength of its style.

From one point of view the two were obviously well-matched, but at the time of their liaison, or at least at its beginning, the advantage was Flaubert's. She was striking, twelve years his senior, and with something of a reputation as a woman of letters. He was the first to see that that reputation was undeserved, but it was his jealous friends, chief among them Maxime du Camp, who missed no opportunity to turn her into an object of ridicule.

Had she not fallen in love with Flaubert, had he not withdrawn from her company, their story might have ended more happily than it did, were it not for one fatal mistake. She told him that she would like to meet his mother. This is a mistake not infrequently made by rather dim women. She went unannounced to Croisset and gave a note to the chambermaid to tell Flaubert of her arrival. Horrified, he joined her, or circumvented her, outside the house, refused to invite her in, and fobbed her off with a promise that he would meet her that evening in Rouen. There he told her that there must be nothing more between them. Yet her value as an ally, as opposed to a mistress, was great enough to impel him to write her over a hundred letters during the composition of *Madame Bovary*, which he began the following year, in 1851. The correspondence continued until 1855, and ended in a letter which is in itself some kind of masterpiece. "Madame: I was told that you took the trouble to come here to see me three times last evening. I was not in. And, fearing that your persistence might provoke me to humiliate you, wisdom leads me to warn you that I shall never be in. I have the honour of saluting you. G.F."

Colet later revealed that she disliked *Madame Bovary*. To justify her opinion it is necessary to remember that in her own eyes, though not

in anybody else's, she was the pre-eminent literary figure. She may
once have even entertained the notion that it was her fame as a woman
of letters that had brought Flaubert to her side. In 1846, when they met
in the studio of the sculptor Pradier, he was a mere twenty-four to her
thirty-six and had published nothing, whereas she was the prolific
author of occasional prose and verse, and had already won the
Académie Française poetry prize twice (she was later to win it a third
time). Yet although she was known to a fairly wide circle, she owes her
historical survival to the massive irony that she was the recipient of
Flaubert's letters, that she is in fact a footnote in Flaubert's life, in spite
of her very real insistence that she occupy centre stage in her own.
It is this injustice that Francine du Plessix Gray attempts to redress,
and she makes a handsome job of it. Even to retrieve Colet from that
famous correspondence is a heroic enterprise. To confer on her a
dignity which survives the undoubted humiliations she was forced to
endure is a generous one, and an achievement which owes something,
but not everything, to a female solidarity which the reader will salute
as touching and endearing.

That Colet had a life of her own is attested not merely by her
numerous writings, which few will consult, but by her lonely and
forthright demeanour, of a kind that confers a reputation, but not
necessarily the esteem to go with it. It should be remembered that in
the course of her arduous passage through Parisian society she had no
assets apart from her remarkable looks, poor capital after the age of
forty. She was to become stout and sickly in her advancing years, yet
the initial impression had been considerable. An artless woman
penning artless verses might have been expected to be an object of
male indulgence, but Colet had been relatively radicalized by a harsh
family and an indifferent husband, and her expectations were high.
She had temperament but no money, whereas money would have
served her better. Unlike her role models she was extremely poor.
When entertaining in the various flats she painted blue to emphasize

the colour of her eyes, she was obliged to save the tea leaves from one reception, to dry them on the window-sill, and to serve them up again the following week. She was also of an ardent and impulsive nature, an easy convert to liberal causes, and in old age a fearless advocate of Italian nationalism.

Yet for all these qualities, and they were considerable, it is impossible to confer on her success as a feminist icon, as her biographer does. Rather is she an exponent of Romantic behaviour, fighting an unequal battle for acclaim in a period best known for its masculine accomplishments. She was not so much a Muse, though that was how she was known, as a confidante of great men: Victor Cousin, Hugo, Musset, Vigny. Yet she lacked a sense of self-preservation: she could have lived with either Cousin or Vigny and been comfortable and cared for. In fact she was fallible, and perhaps less than rational. Perhaps she saw no advantage if her heart were not engaged.

She was born into the provincial nobility at Servanes, in the Alpilles. After her parents died she was effectively disinherited by her brothers and sister and forced to take refuge with her nurse. She married Hippolyte Colet, a music teacher, because he had obtained a post in Paris, and Paris was where she longed to be. She won her first Académie prize in 1839, when she was twenty-seven, a heady start to what she hoped would be an outstanding career. She made useful acquaintances by the simple expedient of sending them her poems; their polite letters of acknowledgement opened the way for an admiring correspondence. Poverty forced her to be opportunistic, although she was never averse to publicity. When the critic Alphonse Karr printed a derogatory remark about her in his journal Guêpes, she went to his house and stabbed him in the back, her arm, as he recounted, "raised in a tragedian's gesture". No harm was done, and he very handsomely went out and called her a cab. She published recklessly and without discrimination: friends, including Flaubert, urged her to be more patient and more severe. Her later years saw her living in Italy, enthralled by the Risorgimento, intercepting Cavour, and demanding an audience with the Pope, informing the French ambassador at what hour she would be free to call on him. Through sheer courage she became formidable, and by an interesting turn of the wheel robustly anti-clerical. Corpulent and ailing, she climbed to the crater of Vesuvius in a crinoline and high-heeled shoes, the soles of which were blackened by the lava. She died in 1876. Her daughter countermanded her wish for a civic burial and she was interred with the full rites of the church she so scorned.

Edmond de Goncourt in his *Journal*, on 19 February 1877: "A remark of Louise Colet's. She said to a friend of a medical student who was her current lover: 'So what's become of your friend? I haven't seen him in more than a fortnight . . . at my age, and with my temperament, do you think that entirely healthy?'" This anecdote is not quoted by Francine du Plessix Gray, yet this aspect of Colet's life and career must have played a considerable part in forming her reputation. It is the part that does not survive. The uninhibited lover that she must have been explains Flaubert's attachment. The confidence she gave him to write those letters to her is another matter. Perhaps she was rather great after all.

20

Scarsdale Romance*

MRS JEAN HARRIS, A trim widow of fifty-six, was a woman who had reason to congratulate herself on making a success of her life. She had risen from undistinguished but respectable suburban beginnings to the position of headmistress of the select Madeira School for girls, in McLean, Virginia. She had married young and had two fine sons. She had kept her looks, and, apart from the occasional bout of depression or fatigue, her health. She was well-respected in the academic world, was an active fund-raiser, and presented to the girls in her charge a picture of independence, decorum, and high moral standards. So high, indeed, were these moral standards that the penalties she inflicted on her girls for such unimportant misdemeanours as drinking beer or smoking marijuana were met with some criticism, not only from the girls themselves but from her colleagues and from the school board. Yet such criticism was powerless to modify Mrs Harris's actions, for it was clear, even to those who did not warm to her, that Mrs Harris was a lady whose behaviour was so impeccable that she expected no less of others. Mrs Harris did not drink beer or smoke marijuana. But she did something else. On the night of 10 March 1980, Mrs Harris took a gun, got into her car, drove for five hours to Westchester, woke her lover of fourteen years, Dr Herman Tarnower, from his sleep, shot him, and left him dying on

*Diana Trilling, *Mrs Harris*. Hamish Hamilton, London. Harcourt Brace Jovanovich, New York. *The London Review of Books*, 6-19 May 1982.

the floor while she went back to her car and began to drive away. She did not intend to escape. In any event the police were already approaching, alerted by Tarnower's housekeeper, Suzanne van der Vreken. Mrs Harris was taken to the police station and in due course brought to trial. She was convicted of murder in the second degree and condemned to serve a sentence of a minimum of fifteen years.

It was thought that Mrs Harris had been driven to this grave act by one particular circumstance. Although apparently resigned to her lover's compulsive philandering, she found it very difficult to bear when he switched his attention from other women to one other woman, Mrs Lynne Tryforos, who was very much younger than Mrs Harris herself. Mrs Harris had the terrible feeling that she was being discarded, that Dr Tarnower, a confirmed bachelor, might indeed marry Mrs Tryforos. What gave her this impression was not only the relative inaccessibility of Dr Tarnower but the knowledge that on 19 April he was to be honoured at a dinner given by the Westchester County Heart Association, and that his partner at the top table was not to be Mrs Harris, his stylish companion of fourteen years, but the very much less distinguished Mrs Tryforos.

Mrs Harris's despair and fear can be imagined. She was not well, was overworked, worn out. Recently, and on more than one occasion, her professional judgement had been called into question. She was tired of the rigorous respectability demanded of her. "I was a person and no one ever knew," she was to write to a colleague. Certainly a woman of her temperament and behaviour must have been in an extremity of suffering to have performed an act so apparently out of character. For it was Mrs Harris's character that was her strongest recommendation. Here was no common or garden killer, it was thought, but a tragic heroine driven to commit the ultimate crime by her desperation and sadness. Until the trial – indeed until the end of the trial and the reading of the only significant document in the case, the Scarsdale Letter – Mrs Harris was perceived to be in some way intrinsically harmless. And at this stage she puts one in mind of one of Henry James's minor characters, Mrs Carrie Donner, who was reported to be "wild". "Wild?" muses James's surrogate silkily. "Why, she's simply tameness run to seed."

Not so Dr Tarnower, rich and celebrated physician, and author of *The Complete Scarsdale Medical Diet*. Dr Tarnower at home might have been invented by Philip Roth, as an honorary member of the Tarnopol or Zuckerman families, the one who makes good, along slightly crossed tribal lines. With his Japanese-style suburban estate, his disaffected Belgian houseman, his appreciation of women half his age, his gourmet dinners, and his genial habit of presenting his guests with an inscribed copy of his diet book – in paperback Tarnower does not cut a convincing figure as the victim in the case. Nor is he attractive enough to gain one's sympathy. Penurious beginnings had exploded into an elaborate and sybaritic style of life which Tarnower greatly enjoyed. He seems to have been a genuine man of pleasure, and thus to have exerted a disagreeable power, for men of pleasure have minimal consciences and fallible memories. The ageing and tiring Mrs Harris was a nuisance to Dr Tarnower. When, as she said, she woke him from his sleep and asked him to kill her with her own gun he was quite simply exasperated. He gripped Mrs Harris's hand or arm in order to stop her shooting herself, and she, involuntarily or reflexively, pulled the trigger. Dr Tarnower sustained one wound in the hand and three in the chest, from which he died shortly afterwards, and, apart from the necessity of establishing the burden of proof, his death seemed to pose a moral problem: whether the sort of woman Mrs Harris was should be allowed to murder the sort of man Dr Tarnower was, with the further implication that she should, in all justice, be able to claim some kind of immunity for having done so.

But what sort of a man was he? He was not one of those mythic characters who inspire in others "the sacred terror" (Henry James again) and whose power over women is acknowledged and indulged, simply because it is a power, and because all men would like to possess it and all women to enjoy it. Tarnower, on the contrary, appears to have been cheap and crass, and to have used women without in the least caring for them. The only indication of his extremely limited interest in any particular woman was the amount of money he was willing to spend on entertaining her, and of course himself. Mrs Harris in her time enjoyed trips to Kenya, Khartoum, Ceylon, Saudi Arabia, Vietnam, Nepal, Bali, Singapore and Russia. By Dr Tarnower's reckoning, therefore, Mrs Harris had thus had a good run for her, or rather his, money. It was all very well for Mrs Harris to protest that he had proposed marriage to her; the proposal had been quickly retracted on the grounds that the doctor was wedded to his profession. Nor did it do her any good to remind him of the hours she had spent working on his diet book, the high intellectual calibre of which can be judged by the report, inserted somewhere between the recipes for Eggs Gitano and Pineapple Surprise Aloha, that a wife and husband "dieting team" had taken up knitting and macramé "to keep our hands busy and out of the snack bowl while watching TV with the kids". None of this cut any ice with Dr Tarnower, who shed his lustre on one woman after another, or, more usually, at the same time, and could not or would not understand their objections when they met at his table or beside his pool or occasionally passed each other in the driveway of his house.

In return for his favours, the women in Dr Tarnower's busy life would be allowed the use of a wardrobe in his "dressing area", and if one mistress found another mistress's clothes there, well, as Dr Tarnower would say, that was her problem. These wretched women would gaily signal their presence to their lover by printing greetings in the *New York Times*, presenting him with engraved gold cufflinks, or, as Mrs Harris did, writing droll verses congratulating him on his long list of conquests. They would be forced into these stratagems because their telephone calls to Dr Tarnower, which were numerous and very frequent, were not always well received. Thus the women would be reduced to telephoning his friends or questioning his servants. Mrs Harris and Mrs Tryforos, of course, telephoned each other, but usually under the cloak of anonymity. Having set in motion the humiliation of these women, in which they undoubtedly colluded, Dr Tarnower usually did what he most liked to do, and retired to bed, early and alone. The most striking thing about him was that he was entirely unmemorable. He aroused the most perverse of passions not because he was unique but because he was unavailable. Once Mrs Harris went on trial for his murder, no one spared him a second thought; he proved, in the eyes of the public, to be as insubstantial as his own affections. Out of sight, he was literally out of mind. He left no ghost behind, no voice from the grave: nothing but the plausible smile of the sexual dilettante. It was for this reason that many women, witnessing the reinstatement of Mrs Harris as the central figure in this drama, and the reduction of Dr Tarnower to what they felt to be his ignominious essence, reckoned that, whatever the verdict, a kind of justice had already been done.

Murder in the second degree involves the conscious intent to kill. But the verdict of the jury was irrelevant to the main issue, and in any event hinged upon a technicality which was neither proved or disproved. What few people can have doubted was Mrs Harris's *unconscious* intent to murder Dr Tarnower, and not merely on the night of 10 March but for months, even years, before that date. It is evident from certain of her remarks to friends or to Dr Tarnower himself that she hated him with the passion of the frustrated lover and the despair of the biologically redundant. She hated him for her loss of judgement, her loss of status, her loss of integrity. The metaphorical truth of Mrs Harris's desire and intent to kill Dr Tarnower was so clear to the thoughtful witness that the tedious deliberations of the courtroom seemed otiose. With this, as it were, prejudged, there is

no paradox involved in the fact that the degradation of the trial left
Mrs Harris almost intact, as if lightened of a burden, yet was experienced by all the other participants, none of whom appears to have
been of a stature suitable to the occasion. Counsel for the defence,
whose father for some reason changed his name from the decent and
recognizable Aronowitz to the hybrid and unpronounceable Aurnou,
wears striped brown suits, and when not making emotional appeals to
the jury, with tears in his eyes, can be seen to turn round and wink at
his wife. Counsel for the prosecution, Bolen, has some difficulty in
framing his questions, and his barbaric use of the language offends the
fastidious Mrs Harris, who corrects his syntax. Uncommunicative
policemen admit, under questioning, that they handled bloodstained
telephones or permitted Mrs Harris to change her bloodstained
blouse. Each medical witness discredits the preceding medical witness.
The judge, Judge Leggett, is not good at keeping order, and after
pronouncing the sentence (minimum fifteen years, maximum life)
delivers himself of this incredible declaration:

> Mrs Harris, in regard to my observation of you,
> I found you to be a brilliant, brilliant woman, and I
> am going to ask this: in regard to Mrs Harris in
> Bedford Hills, my feeling is that she can be a most
> useful person in that facility and help other people.
> Her brilliance can probably bring some light into
> some other women's lives because of any ignorance
> and lack of knowledge. Anything that can be done .
> with respect to giving her the opportunity to help
> her fellow women that are in that prison I would
> like it to be done. I think that she has so much to offer
> the women that are there that not to afford her that
> opportunity would be to deprive society and the
> other inmates in there of a very great advantage and

> a blessing. It's unhappy that you have to be sentenced,
> Mrs Harris, and the best I can say to you, is, *the best
> of luck* [my italics].

And Mrs Harris's behaviour? Diana Trilling observed her to be trim,
neat, busy and affectless. She scribbled notes to her defence counsel,
whom she addressed from the witness-stand as "Joel", she bristled at
certain infelicities of procedure, but at no point did she reveal herself
to be a woman with a broken heart. To Diana Trilling she exhibited
the *belle indifférence* of the psychotic, but it may be that during the
trial Mrs Harris simply had no appropriate emotions available to her.
She had left them all behind, and without regret, for they had been
ugly. Most important of all, she was no longer frightened – frightened
by her envy of the girls in her charge, whose lax and lazy hedonism
she had dealt with so punitively, frightened of her rival, Lynne
Tryforos, who possessed the priceless assets of youth and shamelessness, frightened of the school board which had expressed doubts as to
her suitability to continue as headmistress of Madeira School, frightened of her fatigue, frightened of what might happen to her when she
stopped taking the sedatives which Dr Tarnower prescribed for her
under another name, frightened, above all, of Dr Tarnower, who had
brought her to this pass. By killing him she effectively removed all
her fears. And she removed the cause of them. Towards the end of the
trial she appeared white and tired, but she did not waver in her compo-
sure or in the assertion of her innocence. Whether this was *belle
indifférence* or simply the relief of having taken action at last would
need the competence of quite a different court to decide.

And yet she is unsympathetic. And in addition to that she too is
profoundly undistinguished. A woman who claims to be superior, as
Mrs Harris constantly did, must demonstrate this quality, and must
demonstrate it in sufficient measure to convince others of her particular distinction. But even in adversity superior women do not resort

to the sort of language or reveal the sort of preoccupation made manifest in the long letter Mrs Harris wrote to her lover, never received by him, retrieved, and, after considerable and dramatic delay, produced as evidence in court at a moment during the trial when her steadfast appearance of respectability and the decent sentiments she proclaimed had all but convinced her audience of her worth.

The Scarsdale Letter deals, in rambling and furious fashion, with three matters: with the dinner of 19 April, at which Mrs Harris so strongly desired to be present as Dr Tarnower's partner; with money; and with Lynne Tryforos. The only surprising element in this letter is the fact that Mrs Harris kept such strict mental account of money spent and not spent over the past fourteen years. She protests her financial abasement, her financial sacrifices, her financial modesty, her financial rights. She reminds Dr Tarnower that she let him pick up the bill for a yellow dress of hers only because Lynne Tryforos has smeared it with her shit. She tells him that her children's education could have been improved with a little financial help. And she accuses him, murderously, of replacing her in his will by Lynne Tryforos, who would now stand to gain a quarter of a million dollars, her two daughters twenty-five thousand dollars apiece – "and the boys and me nothing". The fact that Tarnower paid for all their excursions and hotel reservations – a not inconsiderable sum – does not figure in her calculations, nor does the pleasure she has had from them. What she has enjoyed is discounted or forgotten. It is what she has not enjoyed, and what she suspects another woman of enjoying, that unbalances her.

That other woman is referred to, *passim*, as a "vicious adulterous psychotic", "your whore", "your psychotic whore", "your adulterous slut", "a self-serving ignorant slut", "a lying slut", "dishonest, igno-rant, and tasteless". Mrs Harris remarks of her, "Her voice is vomitous to me." Yet such is Mrs Harris's travail that she cannot perceive that these terms might change the doctor's attitude to her. She makes a bargain with him: he can see Lynne in March on condition that he devote April to her, Mrs Harris. The bargain is strengthened: "I give you my word that if you just aren't cruel I won't make you wretched." And as for the Westchester County Heart Association dinner, she assures him that she will be there, "even if the slut comes - indeed I don't care if she pops naked out of a cake with her tits frosted with chocolate".

At this point in the trial, and indeed long after it, the impact of this letter is profound, perhaps more profound than the actual killing, the technical details of which have never been satisfactorily established. It is profound because one has been willing to give Mrs Harris one's sympathy, to a certain extent, exactly on her own terms: that is, on the understanding that she was a lady, and a lady whose delicate sensibilities had been outraged at her rejection in favour of a woman whose manners were coarse and vindictive – a woman, in fact, who was no lady. A lady is perhaps recognizable as a woman who consistently behaves better than she feels like doing. As Diana Trilling remarks, "the idea of a gentleman has to all purposes disappeared from our culture, but not the idea of the lady; the title has been largely discarded but the concept remains." The truly tragic element in the case is Mrs Harris's surrender of her previous moral standards, her genuine fall from grace. And this final degradation – of the refined headmistress, whose "veracity" and "peaceability" were attested by her colleagues, to a raging and foul-mouthed energumen – is the degradation not only of Mrs Harris but of the very concept itself. When the word "lady" is used in the future, it will need to be tested as rigorously as the term honnête homme was at the court of Louis XIV.

And that shambling courtroom, in which everyone appears to have been eating junk food, that ludicrous final speech from the bench – what are we to make of these? What justice could such people do to the defiled puritan that was Mrs Harris, the woman of whose "morbid unimpeachability" Diana Trilling speaks with respect? What are we to make of the fact that the only enlightened witness seems to have been Diana Trilling herself, and what are we to make of the fact that she enshrines her observations in a genre which has been turned to sensational advantage by Truman Capote and Norman Mailer? As a specimen of the genre it is superb, but it has to be said that it is an unsatisfactory, even a morally dubious genre. It is a genre in which Rebecca West had earlier made a faultless showing with her account of the case of Mr Setty and Mr Hume. In stately prose, and with a Dickensian relish for geographical detail and for common speech, West presented this disagreeable case as a sort of curiosity of post-war London. Her account is not without a certain bizarre lightheartedness, even a certain appetite. Her sympathies are never engaged, her insight is thus not brought to bear on the accused, but as a narrative it is recognizably the work of a writer who respects the art of fiction. A different sort of fictive impulse was exercised by Pamela Hansford Johnson, when, reviewing the behaviour of Ian Brady and Myra Hindley, on trial for the Moors Murders, she wrote her thoughts *On Iniquity*. Here was a perception of evil that distorted the more trivial facts, and with it a great fear, and with that fear its not unusual corollary, an indictment of society, the sensation-celebrating society of the Sixties. But Diana Trilling is too sensitive to seek the safety of either haven. And as a woman of conscience she cannot simply content herself with the facts. What is obvious is that a suitable structure for the particular experience she so scrupulously charts is seen to be lacking, perhaps no longer exists.

Diana Trilling is of course aware of this. She complains that contemporary literature – by which she means fiction – does not deal with those high matters of love, grief, revenge, ambition, jealousy, infractions of morality and behaviour so necessary to instruct us in the range of our own feelings and the conduct of our own lives. This is the most valid point she makes in what is by any standards a curious and even a disturbing book. And the omission is not made good: the author is too honest for that. For although the moral conscience is still active in Mrs Trilling, and no doubt in her readers as well, it is working in a context of uneasiness, and, more important, of confusion: the confusion of the familiar with the unfamiliar, of the junk food with the "morbid unimpeachability" of Mrs Harris. Such a confusion would have been viewed as incompetent by any nineteenth-century novelist seeking to make his point. And that is the main difference: Mrs Trilling has no point to make. She charts, with evident discomfort, the shifting of her sympathies. The Mrs Harris whom she hoped to serve as the wronged heroine of a major passion disturbs her, first as a relentless and unsympathetic enigma, bristling with her rights and wrongs, and finally as the victim and perpetrator of a moral outrage. It is a subject which demands the very highest powers, and there are few writers of fiction alive today who could encompass it.

It is clear that men of Dr Tarnower's type are fatal to women like Mrs Harris, whose sexual experience would appear to have been limited and whose awareness of failure extreme. By the same token it cannot be denied that women of Mrs Harris's type are fatal to men like Dr Tarnower, in whom the capacity for emotional loyalty, or even sympathy, appears to have been entirely absent. The conjunction of the two was extraordinary, and of course remains largely unknown. The gaps left by the reportage could only be supplied by the inductive powers of the novelist.

Yet any examination of the implications of human wishes and their effect on human behaviour is welcome, and, as has been indicated, is, in the present state of our customs and beliefs, rather rare. Diana Trilling has written a book which might prove to be, in circumstances as yet unjudged, exemplary.

21

Women Against Men*

*T*HE GOLDEN NOTEBOOK TAKES one back not only in time but in consciousness. It is just twenty years old, and re-read from the standpoint of 1982,[†] it seems to belong to an immensely confusing period, weighed down by the anxieties of a decade that now appears remote, incomprehensible to those for whom the Sixties signify permissiveness, euphoria, liberty and pleasure. It reminds us, among other things, that the Sixties inherited the dilemmas of the Fifties, and made an all too conscious attempt to bury them. Reading *The Golden Notebook* when it first appeared, I remember being impressed by its entirely grown-up seriousness; it connected in my mind with its not dissimilar counterpart in France, Simone de Beauvoir's *Les Mandarins*. Both were concerned, overwhelmingly, with the lives led by thinking women, both in and out of politics; both had to do with loyalty, disillusion, the fragmentation of beliefs formerly held to be indissoluble, and the effects of such fragmentation on the personality. More significantly, both had to do with the paradox of the thinking woman's attitude to love and expectation in her personal life, and it is salutary, and not a little shocking, to reflect on how much has been gained, and how much more lost, in the twenty years of *The Golden Notebook*'s history.

*Doris Lessing, *The Golden Notebook*. Michael Joseph, second edition reissued. *The London Review of Books*, 2-15 September 1982.
[†] The date of this review.

The Golden Notebook sets out to be a *Bildungsroman*, and an attempt to give an accurate picture of mid-twentieth-century England, such as *Le Rouge et le noir* and *Anna Karenina* had set out to do for the France and the Russia of their time. This is Doris Lessing's explicit intention. In a confused and defensive preface, written for the edition of 1972, she states her dissatisfaction with the English tradition and asserts that no nineteenth-century novel by an English writer could claim the same sort of success as that enjoyed by Stendhal and Tolstoy. George Eliot, she finds, is disqualified by her morality.

Doris Lessing is a pioneer of feminist self-consciousness in its raw state, and the very rhythm of her remorseless, circular, and outstandingly honest narrative reflects the essentially inward-looking perceptions of a woman, as opposed to the lineal undertakings of a man. Therefore, instead of writing an up-to-date version of *The Way We Live Now*, she has produced a seminal, almost a clinical work, a novel, perhaps, but certainly not a fiction, in which the heroine represents all that is most terrifying about the female archetype. And having isolated and delineated that archetype, she establishes it as an entity from which latter-day feminists fearfully, hastily, and perhaps cleverly, have done their best to depart. It is an archetype which has as much to do with Freud and Breuer as with the brave new woman fashioned by Germaine Greer and Betty Friedan, yet the liberated woman of today must still contend with it, and measure her success in terms of her ability to do so.

The Golden Notebook was written at a time when women were beginning to have ambitions for self-realization that came into conflict with their traditional roles. It was a time before instructions had been issued on how to combine domestic happiness with career expectations. But by the same token, the desperation of that edict – only combine! – had not yet come to dominate a woman's thinking to the exclusion of other relevant factors in the case. The women in *The Golden Notebook* work because they are independent and slightly eccentric and because it is therefore natural and indeed necessary for them to conduct their lives in this manner. They also need the money, because they are spectacularly unsuccessful at being wives, mothers and mistresses. They attach no emblematic or suffragist importance to the fact that they work and maintain themselves, and to state the position fairly, they hardly work at all by today's standards: Anna, the heroine, is a writer, and her friend Molly is a small-time actress. These two women have a strong and rueful friendship and are never more united than when pointing out the shortcomings of a particular man. In the opening chapter of the book their chosen victim is Molly's former husband, Richard, a vaguely plutocratic figure. They laugh at him: he, quite simply, fails to understand them.

But who could? They both exist at the fag-end of a number of exhausted possibilities. They have both been members of the Communist Party. They have both undergone psychoanalysis. They have agonized their way through apartheid in Africa and the Mau Mau threat, the Czech sabotage trials, the deaths of Stalin and Beria and the revelations subsequent to their demise, the activities of McCarthy and his witch-hunting senators, the perfecting of the H-bomb and the proliferation of H-bomb tests, the enormous increase in defence budget spending and the consequent delay in the implementation of health and social reforms, and Einstein's recognition of the very real possibility of general annihilation. Their concerns are so vast and so important that Richard's exasperation and his preference for his young secretaries are almost forgiveable. These women inherit, from their own intellectual formation, a busyness, a grappling with central issues, a determination to come to grips with the truth, however unpleasant this may be, and also a responsibility for their own motives, a tendency to reify, an ability to dream in symbolic or even political terms, a willingness to mythologize their own predicament, which releases them, slightly shaken, from their past, only to teach them that they have very few guidelines to help them to deal with the future.

Anna, the heroine, is in fact released into chaos, into fragmentation. Anna is the writer, the one whose novel, *Frontiers of War*, has earned her enough to live on and who is now suffering from writer's block, not the sort of block that makes writing impossible but the sort of block that can only produce episodes and cannot conceive of a coherent narrative. In order to overcome this block Anna buys four notebooks with different-coloured covers: a black notebook, which is to do with her life as a writer; a red notebook, concerned with politics; a yellow notebook, "in which I make stories out of my own experiences"; and a blue notebook, which tries to be a diary. This design serves well for much of the book, and it enables Doris Lessing to present impressive and discrete accounts of colonial life in Africa (as part of Anna's own history and the inspiration for her novel), of the latter days of a Party member, of the vague but dawning knowledge that compassion for society may exist outside the Party's programme and structure, and of attempts to write another novel in which Anna will be objectified as Ella and in which Ella will be confronted with those same difficulties which Anna has failed to resolve.

All these devices fail. Ella, the fictional character within the novel, disappears when she comes up against the same problems that beset Anna, the fictional character devised by Doris Lessing. And the device of four separate notebooks fails, as Anna's confusion grows under the weight of the chaotic world in which she finds herself living. But the main threat to Anna, to her precarious sense of order, to her ability to control phenomena by "naming" them, lies in the central problem of her life as a woman: her failure to secure a man's love in terms of the rigorous truthfulness which her experience has taught her to practise and expect, and which is exacerbated by her vocation as a writer, for, as she says, "when I'm writing I seem to have some awful second sight, an intuition of some kind; a kind of intelligence is at work which is much too painful to use in ordinary life; one couldn't use it at all if one used it for living."

Anna also says: "The Russian revolution, the Chinese revolution –
they're nothing at all. The real revolution is women against men." And
there is no doubt that this is the most important and significant aspect
of the book. The paltry Richard fades into the background as more
and more personable and complicated men throng into the foreground: Ella's married lover, Anna's unloved and unregretted
husband, various Pauls and Michaels, and a persistent and disturbing
American character who is called, variously, Nelson or Hank or Milt
or, finally, Saul. These lovers are marked by what Anna perceives as
a typically male abnormality of the personality: in fact Saul is so
abnormal that he threatens Anna's own sanity, although it must be
said that that sanity has already been breached by the enormous dismay Anna experiences as she comes to recognize the incompatibility
that exists between men and women.

These love affairs are failures, and they fail for reasons which are
demonstrably important. In her search for a truthful union, Anna, the
emancipated and independent woman, comes up against the phenomenon of a certain kind of male anxiety, which is in effect a fear of
engulfment. For a man dominated or circumscribed by this anxiety,
it would seem that the greatest victory is to make love to a woman (or
to be thought to be making love to her – a device used by Saul to
arouse Anna's jealousy) and then to get away. Anna perceives that
there is a certain male ethic which decrees this to be right: such behaviour will ensure a man credit in the eyes of his peers, and, more
important, it will safeguard what he feels to be his essential integrity.
Such a man will make an initial and proprietory raid on a woman but
will turn away once he has elicited the maximum response, for it is
precisely this maximum response which he neither wants nor needs.
As Anna says, in one of those insights which leap off the page: "with
my intelligence I knew that this man was repeating a pattern over and
over again: courting a woman with his intelligence and sympathy,
claiming her emotionally; then, when she began to claim him in

return, running away. And the better a woman was, the sooner he began to run."

Anna cannot solve this problem. The repetition and confusion in this section of the book, which is the penultimate section, are imprinted with madness and despair. Yet Anna knows that when her daughter comes home from school she will revert to being a normal, cheerful, and reliable figure. Traditional expectations will have triumphed over the penalites of thinking and feeling beyond the expected norms, and if there is further matter for scrutiny here it is left undisturbed. The book ends with a symbol and an anticlimax. Saul and Anna agree to part, each bidding the other write a novel. Anna goes out and buys another notebook, the golden notebook of the title. The adjective "golden" implies some sort of omniscience or perfection, as in Golden Legend, Golden Bough, Golden Section, and it may be that Anna intends the final notebook to contain a summary or overview. But Saul wants it, and after a short struggle Anna gives it to him. He uses it to write a short political novel which, we are told, does well. Anna goes round to see her friend Molly and finds her about to marry a wealthy Hampstead businessman. Anna herself decides to get a job, probably in welfare or social work. No irony is intended here: it is as if exhaustion or "working through" has bought about a certain practical sense of what is possible.

What follows from this given, and remorselessly examined, dilemma of "women against men" is, perhaps indirectly, a recognition and a compromise. In much popular writing today on feminist matters, and indeed in Betty Friedan's *The Second Stage*, there is an uneasy line of thinking which proposes that the proper companion for the liberated woman is the excessively uxorious man, the man who shares the burdens of housekeeping and child-rearing, so that his wife or partner is free to pursue her career and interests on equal terms. However, it must be conceded that, except in the sphere of domestic arrangements, the uxorious man may be precisely the man least likely to satisfy the imaginative requirements of the liberated woman. This is the dilemma which has succeeded the admittedly harsher dilemma at the heart of *The Golden Notebook*. This is the way we live now.

At this point it might be salutary to refer to Trollope's masterpiece, if only to measure the enormous distance that separates the traditional norms of the nineteenth century from the expansive thinking of the twentieth, with particular reference to matters of love and longing. Here is Trollope:

> The man had no poetry about him. He did not even care for romance. All the outside belongings of love which are so pleasant to many men and which to women afford the one sweetness in life which they really relish were nothing to him. There are both men and women to whom even the delays and disappointments of love are charming, even when they exist to the detriment of hope. It is sweet to such persons to be melancholy, sweet to pine, sweet to feel that they are now wretched after a romantic fashion as have been those heroes and heroines of whose sufferings they have read in poetry. But there was nothing of this with Roger Carbury. He had, as he believed, found the woman that he really wanted, who was worthy of his love, and now, having fixed his heart upon her, he longed for her with an amazing longing. He had spoken the simple truth when he declared that life had become indifferent to him without her. No man in England could be less likely to throw himself off the Monument or blow out his brains. But he felt numbed in all the joints of his mind with sorrow. He could not make one thing bear upon another, so as to console himself after any fashion.

There was but one thing for him: to persevere until he got her, or till he had finally lost her. And should the latter be his fate, as he began to fear that it should be, then, he would live, but live only, like a crippled man.

And Doris Lessing, on the fantasy of the third person:

If I were to write this novel, the main theme or motif would be buried at first and only slowly take over. The motif of Paul's wife – the third. At first Ella does not think about her. Then she has to make a conscious effort not to think about her. This is when she knows her attitude towards this woman is despicable: she feels triumph over her, pleasure that she has taken Paul from her. When Ella first becomes conscious of this emotion she is appalled and so ashamed she buries it, fast. Yet the shadow of the third grows again, and it becomes impossible for Ella not to think. She thinks a great deal about the invisible woman to whom Paul returns (and to whom he will always return), and it is now not out of triumph, but envy. She envies her. She slowly, involuntarily, builds up a picture in her mind of a serene, calm, unjealous, unenvious, undemanding woman, full of resources of happiness inside herself, yet always ready to give happiness when it is asked for. It occurs to Ella (but much later, about three years on) that this is a remarkable image to have developed, since it does not correspond at all to anything Paul says about his wife. So where does the picture come from? Slowly Ella understands that this is what she would like to be herself, this imagined woman is her own shadow, everything she is not. Because by now she knows and

is frightened of her utter dependence on Paul. Every
fibre of herself is woven with him and she cannot
imagine living without him.

My feeling here is one of loss rather than gain: loss of honour, loss
of virtue, loss of unity. And there is also a loss of simplicity, which is
apparent in the clarity of Trollope's writing and the complexity of Mrs
Lessing's. Yet she did not invent the contemporary woman, any more
than Trollope invented the gentleman: they simply invented them in
literature. And having once been invented, it was inevitable that such
prototypes should become part of the collective thinking. There
can be no doubt that both these books are extremely important,
Mrs Lessing's awesome exploration no less than Trollope's sturdy and
uncompromising narrative. Trollope went on to write an equally
sturdy autobiography. Mrs Lessing returned to *The Golden Notebook* in
1972, to write a preface. The world had moved on in the ten years that
had elapsed. It had seen the student uprisings of 1968, events of which
Mrs Lessing speaks with warm approval. Unity, except in the most
temporary, political sense, looked even less possible. And in this
preface Mrs Lessing herself seems to betray traces of the old dialectic.
In one paragraph she praises the breakdown of subjectivity and its
replacement by the understanding of self as microcosm ("growing up
is after all only the understanding that one's unique and incredible
experience is what everybody shares"), and in the next she laments as
painful the absence of the intelligent critic: "Why should he (the
writer) expect this extraordinary being, the perfect critic (who does
occasionally exist), why should there be anyone who comprehends
what he is trying to do? After all, there is only one person spinning that
particular cocoon, only one person whose business it is to spin it." Her
concern is, increasingly, freedom from constraint, and if this involves
a break with or from tradition, acceptance, or the control of reason,
the gain in truth will be assumed to be adequate compensation.

Hence, perhaps, her impatience with the morality of George Eliot. Hence too her emulation of Stendhal, who quotes, on the title page of *Le Rouge et le noir*, Danton's dictum, *"La vérité, l'âpre vérité."* It can be said that the truths contained in *The Golden Notebook* are indeed harsh. It can also be said that these particular truths have not been examined in so rigorous and exemplary a fashion since the first appearance of this extraordinary book, in the remote and already misrepresented days of 1962.

22

God's Great Wager*

ALL WE KNOW ABOUT Job is that he dwelt in the land of Uz and that he was in a prosperous way of business. He owned 7,000 sheep, 3,000 camels, 500 yoke of oxen, and a very large household. Apart from these precise and impressive details, we have no information, but we are allowed to form an impression of patriarchal ease, little labour, and tremendous seigneurial enjoyment. Parties are given by the sons, word is sent over to the daughters, and feasting takes place for several days. Such a life is apt to give offence.

One day, in Heaven, "the sons of God came to present themselves before the Lord, and Satan came also amongst them". First problem. Who are these persons? Satan we know, although interestingly enough he has not yet assumed his unique position, and is referred to as "the Satan", or, in this excellent translation, "the Adversary". But the sons of God? Are they angels, and is Elihu, the fourth and unexplained comforter, one of them? Are we to imagine a sort of Olympus, with mild discourse taking place among equals, under the chairmanship of Jupiter? Certainly God behaves in as impulsive and irrational a way as Jupiter, with the same penchant for cunning transformations and the same tremendous rapport with the animal world. The "Adversary" seems tame in comparison, an only slightly

* The Book of Job. A new translation according to the traditional Hebrew text. With introductions by Moshe Greenberg, Jonas C. Greenfield and Nahum M. Sarna. The Jewish Publication Society of America. *The Times Literary Supplement*, 26 December 1980.

discredited member of this gathering, allowed constant access and treated with some amusement and courtesy. It is probably helpful at this point to remember that the writing (or various writings) of this epic is (or are) coeval with certain Greek beliefs and dates from the fourth or fifth century BC. The indication that there are different hands at work can be seen in the widely acknowledged theory that the prologue and the epilogue, in prose, are lifted from some earlier folk tale, and that the happy ending, in particular, is a literary and not a theological device, designed to bring the story to a sym-metrical conclusion, and beyond this worthless, or at best allegorical in content.

Second problem. God and Satan join in a wager to shake Job's faith and unseat his undoubted piety. That this is the prerogative of celestial beings no one doubts; as theology it is suspect, for if the wager gets out of hand, the explanations become irrelevant, and the nature of the wager, indeed the very fact of the wager, can never be revealed to Job himself. Job is not only wronged, he is duped, and in order to justify Himself before Job God is forced to redefine His functions and attributes. In the course of this interest-ing and not altogether painless process Job is completely forgotten; by this time he is presumably so weak that he can no longer curse the day on which he was born, the terrible and basic impiety which may indeed have incurred God's sudden irruption of anger, His transformation into a whirlwind, and His blast of scorn and contempt for Job's predicament. But that is an alternative reading. Third problem.

God gives Satan permission to scourge Job but to spare his life (for there is as yet no life after death). One day Job's sons are having one of their feasts and the roof caves in, killing the lot. Job falls down and praises God, and God offers this to Satan as proof of Job's perfect understanding. Satan replies that a man will suffer anything as long as he himself is left intact, and the second stage of Job's ordeal is set in motion: he is smitten with boils, and his philosophy immediately disappears. Unfortunately, at this moment his three friends turn up, ostensibly to sit down with him and observe the ritual seven days of mourning. They find him distressingly preoccupied with his own situation and are shocked into remonstrance. When they hear him curse the day of his birth and long for death, they launch, severally, into their own confused and restricted theology. Eliphaz the Temanite makes the fundamental but only too understandable mistake of introducing the principle of reward and punishment: "Whoever perished, being innocent? or where were the righteous cut off?" Having said this, he is without explanation for the various ills that befall man, and can only adduce that "man is born to trouble as the sparks fly upward". Eliphaz the Temanite is not an entirely stupid man, for part of his comforting or confession has to do with the magnitude of God, which is the position both of Job and of God Himself. But Eliphaz the Temanite goes on to make the pious mistake of assuming that God, being great, will not smite the innocent. This proves to Job that Eliphaz the Temanite is not up to the profound investigation that is being undertaken, with many twists and turns, in this particular parable.

Bildad the Shuhite, a more rancorous character, observes that no pain is undeserved, and that Job must be wicked without knowing it. "Doth God pervert judgement?" Bildad the Shuhite is also of the tedious opinion that suffering ennobles and that Job will reap great benefits from his experience. Job is clearly prepared to deal with this one; he continues to praise the magnitude of God, but cannot understand His indifference. It also, in the course of his answer to Bildad the Shuhite, becomes apparent to him that God is beyond causality, that anyone can be punished without reason, that the just can suffer immeasurably an undeserved hardship. "If I be wicked, woe unto me, and if I be righteous, yet will I not lift up my head. I am full of confusion; therefore see thou mine affliction." Job begs to be delivered, and indeed sees annihilation as the only deliverance.

But he is condemned to listen to Zophar the Naamathite, who appears to think that all would be clear if only God would explain His purpose, that there is indeed a purpose, but that only God can reveal it. Zophar the Naamathite, a timid and obviously pious man, abjures Job to hope and prepare for the day of his rejoicing, which will surely come.

Job, incensed, replies that he knows all this as well as his friends do, but his problem is that he cannot understand God's purpose in this particular case. Who can? Job's humble desire is to present his case to God and to exact an explanation, and he thereby puts himself in the classic position of all believers whose faith is shaken. He cannot understand the silence of God, and by the same token he cannot tolerate the loquacity of his companions. In the face of God's continued silence Job can only desire death, for the torment of the unexplained is too much for him, particularly as his piety is undiminished. Indeed, as Eliphaz the Temanite weighs in again, Job's very confusion is beginning to tell against him, and no clear answer can be adduced from his situation, which, it should be remembered, is the result of a wager. There is as yet no theological explanation to deal with the concealed, the unexplained, the arbitrary. The disputation between Job and his comforters is far in advance of that between God and Satan. Job, who refuses to renounce God, is already having to reason for Him and beyond Him: an intolerable position which strains the endurance not only of Job himself but of the comforters, who have now been left far behind, with the pious platitudes, not all of them untenable, that come so readily to those who are as yet untried. "Miserable comforters are ye all."

Job's not unnatural defence against his friends is to describe in even greater detail the extent of his sufferings, thus provoking Bildad the Shuhite to even more shocked remonstrance. At this point Job utters as much of a blasphemy as his piety will allow, and saves himself,

at the last minute, by stating that he knows that his Redeemer liveth –
but given the scale of his afflictions this is something of a wager in
itself. Job defines himself as existing in the light of the unreason of
God, and is emboldened to do so in the hope that the ultimate
dialogue will yet take place. But Zophar the Naamathite, poor fellow,
still insists that the wicked are to be put down, that the just man will
triumph. It is clear that the comforters are convinced that Job is
among the wicked, that he is wicked without knowing it, that God
knows that Job is wicked, and that Job himself is either obstinate or
unenlightened.

The terrible passage that follows is a description of Job's doubt,
for it is clear to him that the wicked do flourish. His most urgent
desire is to have this explained to him *by God Himself*; his most intolerable problem is that he cannot order his own case. "Oh, that
I knew where I might find him! that I might come even to his seat."
But God is no longer in His accustomed place. "Behold, I go forward,
but he is not there; and backward, but I cannot perceive him." God
has become inaccessible, a new experience for Job, who formerly
would have agreed with his friends in their reasoning. Whether he
has advanced spiritually by virtue of his dilemma is not made apparent; the tone of the narrative is wilder and more desperate as the
dilemma is left unresolved. Yet Job still persists in proclaiming his
own integrity, and indeed the glory of Job, his qualification for
sanctity (and there is a church in Venice dedicated to San Giobbe)
is this very persistence not only of belief but of personal dignity.
In the midst of his self-abasement Job cannot see where he has
sinned. He recalls the days of his splendour and his uprightness:
"I was eyes to the blind, and feet was I to the lame." The tone of
this passage is markedly more refreshing than the dreary assump-
tions of the comforters. For Job regrets his happiness and does not
conclude that he has sinned. His position is correct, for he still knows
nothing of the wager.

Fourth problem. There now steps upon the scene a fourth comforter named Elihu, who purports to be very young, and, being young, and possibly an angel, or one of the "sons of God", is allowed to be kindled to wrath. Elihu's innovation is to establish that God does not render accounts. There will be no explanation. But, says Elihu, confusingly, God is without wickedness. (How does he know this if there is no explanation?) He also proclaims the autonomy of God, and here he may be getting nearer to a theologically acceptable truth. He thirdly proclaims the unknowable nature of God, a useful point to establish in view of God's subsequent behaviour, and one which indicates that Elihu is uttering the prologue to God's outburst, long delayed, in the final chapters of the book. Elihu also advances the teleological argument in favour of God (He makes the clouds gather, the rain to fall, etc.), and the scene is now set for God's appearance.

God chooses to come in the shape of a whirlwind, either because He is enraged by the banality of the dialogue to which presumably He has been listening, or to divert attention from His previous absence. God launches into a florid, brilliant, and apparently irrelevant celebration of His own activities and authorship; irrelevant, that is, to any of Job's questions, and to his most pressing need for a dialogue. God establishes a *monologue* for all time, challenging Job to say whether he can produce such marvels as the hippopotamus (Behemoth) or the whale (Leviathan), whether he can claim to create anything as wonderful as the horse ("He saith among the trumpets Ha, ha . . ."), the peacock, the unicorn, the spring rains and the eagle. It should be noted that this is a universe without man, and that God is thereby imposing His awe rather than offering an explanation, which, given the origin of the enterprise, is quite understandable.

God indeed is either parading His marvels in order to obfuscate the fact that He is not prepared to answer questions, or He is doing something far more advanced and fruitful: He is proclaiming the splendour and intricacy of the universe and the integrity of every created thing. From this it follows that God is consubstantial with His creation, that Job was correct in stressing his own perfection, and that instead of concentrating on his distressing condition and vainly demanding explanations which, it is clear, will not be forthcoming, he would do better to contemplate the world beyond his dungheap, and to worship God with wonder. And also with fear. For God demands an unconditional worship, beyond causality, beyond reward, beyond understanding. Job, by this reasoning, is condemned to go uncomforted.

Job, in fact, is forgotten as God is forced into a justification of His authority. From being the tribal, familial, patriarchal God of the prologue, the God who rewarded uprightness with sheep and oxen and sons and daughters, He becomes the miraculous, imperious and unknowable God who is not above demonstrating his powers, in a fashion reminiscent of more primitive deities. Yet the concept of the unknowable God, of the random and inexplicable catastrophes that are visited upon His creatures, continues to be the central spiritual problem for all those who proclaim His goodness. And if God felt the need to send a hostage into the world it was surely to reintroduce the concept of mercy, so blatantly lacking in this parable, for it must be remembered that the happy ending – more sheep, more oxen, more sons and daughters – is a poetic device, and one without which the dangerous despair evinced by Job would be unmodified, and no doubt contagious.

For the undoubted hero of the story is Job himself, and God, for all that He created the peacock and the unicorn, for all that He can draw out Leviathan with an hook, does not fully justify His earlier indulgence to Satan. This God does not protect His creatures. But Job has been proved, and has passed his ordeal gloriously. Previously he had heard of God; now he sees. "I have heard of thee through the hearing of the ear but now mine eye seeth thee." Something has taken place, something mysterious and incommunicable, and he abases himself before this new God. Rather a pity, as God now reverts to His previous state of unjustifiable indignation and strikes the three comforters with His wrath. He then reverts to His earlier tribal status and finds it quite in order that Job should intercede for his friends through the medium of a burnt offering of seven bullocks and seven rams. Further regression takes place, and God becomes once more the God of causality who punishes evildoers and rewards the righteous Job with better friends, money, and even more sheep (14,000), camels (6,000), 1,000 yoke of oxen and 1,000 she-asses. More than this: seven more sons and three more daughters are born. These three daughters, who are named, are not only very beautiful; it is specifically stated that they are given inheritance, whereas formerly they could only have aspired to dowries. Job lived to be 140, and saw four generations of his family. This is the perfect imagined ending, and it concludes with the perfect sentence: "So Job died, being old and full of days."

If I have quoted from the Authorized Version it is because it conveys so well the sense of argument and affirmation which are the essence of the story. It must now be said that this new translation from the received Hebrew text is clear and unusually harmonious. That so simple a reading is the work of a committee is something of a marvel in itself. The modest and exemplary introductory paragraphs establish the major facts: that an ancient myth was incorporated into a theological parable, that the text was edited and partly composed by a practised literary hand, and that the time at which the story is supposed to have taken place is very remote, a time of nomadic tribes without shrines or priests. In his chapter on Job's theology Professor Greenberg does not shirk the fact that Job's misfortunes are unjustified and unjustifiable, but proposes that the story is about the survival of faith when both the natural and the divine economy are overturned. It is acknowledged that God is not reasonable, that the numinous is more persuasive than a rational moral order. Once Job ceases to demand accountability he is saved.

But he still knows nothing of the wager. In this respect, as in too many others, God remains unknowable. The plangent message is the longing for certainty. Whether Job's position is strengthened by being miraculously reversed, whether his migivings are appeased by God's eventually giving tongue, in however oblique a fashion, whether the phrase "but now mine eye seeth" refers to something not apparent in the text, cannot be answered in any manner sanctioned by either tradition or custom. It is a book for both believers and unbelievers: a wise, subtle, and terrible parable, and a key text for those in crisis.